I0081392

EMERGENCE

INSPIRING STORIES OF FINDING VALUE IN LIFE'S CONTRAST

Amie Solomon   Anna Dawson
Carmel Charlesworth   Debra Nathanson
Dr. Tricia Working   Elle Embers   Ellie Blake
Georgie Hansen   Jemma Redman
Nyree Johnson   Paulina Smith
Sonja Martinovic   Tina Knittel   Tori Packer

m.

Emergence © Copyright 2024 Mosaic Media

All rights reserved. Apart from any fair dealing for the purposes of research or private study, or criticism or review, as permitted under the Copyright, Design and Patents Act 1988, this publication may only be reproduced, stored or transmitted, in any form or by any means, with the prior permission in writing of the copyright owner, or in the case of the reprographic reproduction in accordance with the terms of licensees issued by the Copyright Licensing Agency. Enquiries concerning reproduction outside those terms should be sent to the Publisher.

Book Cover Design – Naomi Birmingham and Mosaic Media

Editing by Georgia Hansen [Mosaic Media]

Interior Layout – Mosaic Media

For more information, email publishing@mosaic-media.co

ISBN: 978-0-6456887-2-6

Disclaimer

This book is sold with the understanding that the authors are not offering specific personal advice to the reader. For professional advice, seek the services of a suitable qualified practitioner. The authors and publisher disclaims any responsibility for liability, loss or risk, personal or otherwise, that happens as a consequence of the use and application of any of the contents of this book.

Although the publisher and authors have made every effort to ensure the information in this book was correct at press time and while this publication is designed to provide accurate information in regard to the subject matter covered, the publisher and authors assume no responsibility for errors, inaccuracies, omissions, or any other consistencies herein and hereby disclaim any liability to any party for any loss, damage or disruption caused by errors or omissions, whether such errors or omissions results from negligence, accident or any other cause.

The ideas, concepts and opinions expressed in this book are intended to be used for educational purposes only. This book is offered with the understanding that the author or publisher is not rendering medical advice of any kind, nor is the book intended to replace medical advice, to diagnose, prescribe, or treat any condition, illness, or injury.

Content warning: This book contains stories of death, grief, loss, suicide, or suicidal ideation or tendencies. It is important that anyone who is struggling mentally or emotionally proceed with caution. We are not encouraging this behavior of the reader. Content not suitable for readers under the age of 16.

Some names may have been altered to protect privacy.

Dedication

This book is dedicated to the guiding lights of some of the authors in this book.

Allan Stewart, Amelia Hansen, Brett Redman, Harrison Paewhenua, Jake Dawson, Dr. John Moran, Karen-Lea Alexander, Lola Solomon, Luka Martinovic, Slobodanka Pavlovic, and Warren James Fink.

Are you ready to publish your book?

We are here to help women become the Author of their life, not just their book.

Our unique book strategy helps women not just share their message with the world, but starts the movement, creates the legacy and builds the dream business they desire.

This book method acts as an entire marketing channel, bringing in daily book sales and dream clients!

Are you ready to turn your message into a book that continues to work FOR you?

Visit www.mosaicmediaco.as.me to schedule a dream book session today, where we can ideate you book, and run through our strategy and see if it's something you and your business is ready for. Visit www.mosaic-media.co to learn more.

Contents

Introduction

During a masterclass at the end of last year (2023) with a very well-known, big name in the coaching industry, Melanie Ann Layer, who is known for her luxe vibes and unparalleled out-of-this-world thought leadership, she said something that stuck with me.

"Seek to find the value in the contrast of life," and therein lies our true currency. It's how we *perceive* our experiences that brings us freedom, not our experiences themselves.

That is when the idea for this book landed.

I have been living by this notion for the past several years, since the loss of my daughter.

And Melanie had summed it up in a few sentences. Our true currency is in finding the value in what is truly important to us, and shifting our perspective to receive the value in it all, even the contrast.

I knew right in that moment there must be other women out there who had found the magic in the tragic and who were living walking exemplars, that there was beauty in the muck of life.

I knew that these women had found so much value, and I could feel their yearning to share this calling to share that value they had found.

Emergence is a book showcasing those women who effortlessly came into my life after I decided to create this book. These are their messages and stories of how they found value in life's greatest contrasts and how they found their way through the darkness to find their own light.

This book is meant to inspire and empower you, the reader, to seek the value in your own contrasting experiences.

It is meant to show you that no matter what you have walked through or are walking through, there is always an opportunity to take that experience and turn it into your greatest gift.

As you read these chapters, I'd love to invite you to do something a little different with the goal of shifting your perspective:

- Think about where in your life you have experienced something unexpected that had the potential to rock your world.

- Take out a journal and write down what you can remember about this experience. The time, the place, the environment, the people involved, and the feelings you had leading up to, during, and afterward.

- Then, I would love for you to go deeper.

  - Did this experience change you for the better or worse?

  - What was the key thing you learned from this experience? Has this learning become something you share with others so they, too, can understand the lesson or message?

  - Has your perspective been shifted from this experience, or is there space for you to further shift your perspective to one of gratitude?

- As you journal this out, notice the narrative or perspective from which you are witnessing this experience. Is it one of abundance or scarcity, fear or love? Is there space for you to shift your perspective into one of a higher frequency?

After you've finished journaling, I wonder how many words you've written and how quickly you were able to get it out of your heart onto paper.

Perhaps think about whether this could be a chapter in your book of life that you would like to share with others.

If it is, maybe you, too, are ready to become the **Author of your life.**

The Grand Reset: A Journey of Overcoming

By Amie Solomon

There's a profound sense of empowerment in rising from the lowest, most life-shattering point of your existence, riddled with anxiety and depression, to breaking through the barriers of fear and awakening to a life of light, peace, and hope.

When approached to co-write this book 'Emergence,' I reflected on the various challenges that led to my personal emergences—the end of a relationship, job losses, significant physical and mental health challenges, and baby loss.

Uttering these trials aloud made it clear: they all played a part in strengthening and guiding me to the fundamental moments where I earnestly embraced living again.

Throughout "The Grand Reset," you will discern the moments I emerge from the shadows of adversity time and again. My life's experiences, both good and bad, bring me to the pivotal point where, instead of succumbing to fear and bewilderment over life's uncertainties, I break through, embracing a newfound trust.

For me, you will hear that my trust resides in my faith, in God. While your higher power might take various forms—be it the universe, angels, your own power, or other religious beliefs—I've witnessed firsthand the transformative influence of both faith and trust, learning to walk confidently in my divine plan even when the ground beneath me turns to quicksand, or I find myself lost at a crossroad.

I learned that one of the most difficult challenges in the aftermath of any traumatic experience is resisting the grip of fear, guilt, and grief. I'm not advocating for suppressing these emotions; instead, I emphasize the importance of not succumbing to and over-accommodating them. Doing so can jeopardize opportunities and numb even the joyous emotions yet to come in the only life we have. When we opt for resilience through trusting the process, we unlock incredible avenues for growth, diverse experiences, and a more complete, enjoyable existence.

Now, allow me to share how I emerged from life's darkest moments, breaking chains and discovering my path to embracing and emerging into this transformative power of trust, hope, faith, and belief.

It all began with my first encounter with emergence. Remember that old saying, 'When it rains, it pours?' Well, I sure experienced a downpour. From the abrupt, unexpected conclusion of a long-term relationship to redundancy in a job I had held for over 15 years, and as if that weren't enough, my lease was up, and my car broke down with a repair cost exceeding the car's value, all within a couple of months. My daily routine, and all that was familiar, was ripped out from underneath me.

Consequently, I found myself grappling with severe anxiety attacks and depressive episodes full of worry and dread about the future, confused as to who I was now in these uncharted waters. Once a confident extrovert, I was now surrendering to a life previously unknown, confined within four walls, trapped in my head, and finding comfort in very few people.

Sitting in my new, empty apartment, feeling sorry for myself and wasting time staring at the TV, I eventually accepted that things wouldn't improve unless I took action and started moving.

After all, GOD can't steer a stationary vehicle, right? We can't make change without making change. So, within 48 hours, I booked a solo trip to Hawaii and Canada for months. I called my parents, told them I was leaving, found an apartment, and left within 72 hours. Why so sudden? I didn't want to give that voice in my head any weight. The one that told me to stay and mourn what was but was no more.

Upon arrival, I ascended to the apartment. As I set down my suitcase and surveyed this unfamiliar place, the severity of what I had done hit me. I'd never been alone like this, especially with such self-doubt about who this version of me was. Overwhelmed, I collapsed onto the bed in tears and remained in that state for a couple of hours. At that moment, I contemplated staying in bed for the entire time.

The turning point arrived when a brilliant ray of light streamed through my window—distracting me just enough to open my eyes to its warmth. Summoning every ounce of strength within me, I managed to stand up.

Without bothering to change out of my travel clothes, I hastily reached for my earphones, cranked up the volume on my music, and headed out the door, leaving behind an untouched suitcase and the indentation of a despondent girl on the bed.

As I closed the door, I felt sure there was a purpose for me being here, something I needed to discover. From that moment onward, my sole objective of this trip was to keep moving, allowing myself to carry my broken heart without letting it break me.

I convinced myself that remaining stagnant would change nothing, so I kept going even when I didn't feel like it. Embracing newfound spontaneity every morning, I randomly chose a direction and embarked on aimless walks, trusting what the day would bring and who would show up. Gradually, I began striking up conversations with fellow tourists, couples, and families, who graciously invited me to join their outings. I joined tours, had dinners with others, and cherished my moments alone.

It was an immensely transformative experience. Each day, I consciously decided to don my armor, shedding the weight of the past and allowing excitement for the future and its boundless possibilities to envelop me, all while standing securely behind the shield of trust in my faith.

You see, I had become enveloped in darkness; I risked missing out on the brilliance life had to offer—a richness I discovered on my journey and the profound rediscovery of myself. Stagnating in obscurity, I might never have found my way back to my true path because, unlike Little Red Riding Hood, I didn't merely stray off my path to pick flowers; I embarked on an expedition far from my track, prompting the divine to intervene. Clearly, a significant reset was necessary to guide me back to where I truly belonged and what I deserved.

Finding the silver lining, let alone understanding its significance, can be challenging for anyone amidst turmoil. However, reflecting a few years later, I realized that the crumbling of my life then was a vital purge. I was in a relationship that demanded a facade, urging me to shape myself into someone I wasn't designed to be. Simultaneously, my workplace had turned toxic, prioritizing profit over ethics, conflicting with my moral compass. Even my ostentatious car, with its flashy exterior, contradicted my humble values.

***

Fast-forward to today: my husband, the love of my life and father of my children, brings light to each day, revealing the moments I might have overlooked and the alternate world I could have found myself in had it not been for those upheavals. Gratitude fills me, knowing our paths may never have crossed without those tumultuous times.

Hindsight in itself is an emergence. I realize that time in my life was essential for my growth. What was lost was never meant for me. When I couldn't discern this truth, trust played a pivotal role—trust in the unseen, in the emergence of a brighter path. Standing here now, I embody confidence, self-love, and authenticity—qualities lost along the way. I owe it all to trusting the process, believing what is meant to be will find its way to me. This process is what I call 'The Grand Reset'—the shedding of the old to welcome the new—learning from the past and trusting that within every upheaval lies the seed of transformation.

Now unfolds the second and most profound emergence that would reshape my very existence. It begins with the dreaded phone call—the gut-wrenching news that shattered our world: the loss of our first baby, our precious Lola, at 18 weeks gestation. Life suddenly felt unbearably unjust. Days blurred into nights as I lay on the floor, pleading for a miracle, questioning why me. Why did my prayers seem to go unanswered?

In the aftermath, my faith and newfound trust in the divine plan faced its ultimate test. The agony of loss consumed me; I couldn't fathom the depth of pain I had been dealt. A few weeks after giving birth to my angel Lola, who came into this world without breath, the despair lingered, keeping me bound to my bed. It was a despair so profound it felt as though my heart was literally tearing apart. Yet, amidst the darkness, a flicker of familiarity emerged—a memory of my first emergence, of trusting in something beyond myself. That recollection sparked a breakthrough. I realized I was being held as I had been supported before, even when I couldn't see it. While I couldn't change the past, I refused to let despair define my future. I had to welcome trust once more, knowing that it was the only way forward.

As a familiar face on an Australian TV show, my husband and I were given the platform to share our story of loss on a prominent television show and in various well-known magazine articles. The flood of messages that followed, seeking support, truly opened my eyes. I realized I *was a significant part of my daughter's divine plan*—to make a difference in others' lives. Through her passing and my courage in speaking about it, I could offer support to those experiencing similar heartbreak, raise awareness, and provide more assistance to grieving parents. Amidst my own sorrow, I discovered a purpose that extended beyond my personal pain, connecting me to a broader narrative of healing and hope.

I realized that it's not just about my divine path; it's also about the paths of others we intersect with. We are like chess pieces, positioned in front, next to, and sometimes on a collision course with many souls in this life. We are all interconnected in facilitating each other's growth, transitions, feelings, and evolution—an unspoken contract signed between us all before entering this world.

In the three years that followed, our two precious boys graced us with their presence. Today, I cannot imagine life without them, a reality that would have been non-existent had we not endured such loss. Their boundless love enriches my world beyond measure, and my appreciation for my healthy children is infinite.

***

An ECG mirrors life's highs and lows, showing our heartbeat's rhythmic fluctuations. Despite craving stability, these fluctuations signify our vitality. Without them, life would cease. As my life continued to present significant challenges, like the ups and downs of an ECG, I found ample opportunities to contemplate my path of growth and renewal in my emergence experiences. With each trial, I gained more control. Both my boys were born during the Covid era, a terrifying time for anyone, especially a bereaved parent with newborns.

Furthermore, between the births of both boys, my husband and I experienced the loss of three babies due to recurrent miscarriages. My youngest was born with persistent breathing issues, leading to numerous hospital stays, and my eldest even stopped breathing on a flight. I endured 13 rounds of mastitis, with the thirteenth time nearly claiming my life as it turned septic. I was so sick I drafted a goodbye email to my husband and boys. Clearly, I survived; otherwise, I'd be giving new meaning to the term 'Ghost Writer...'.

Not only did I survive, but the mastitis and sepsis also served as critical signals that something wasn't right in my breasts, lifting barriers and veils and revealing the true importance, priorities, and fragility of life. Furthermore, it forced my hand to remove my implants, which I intuitively felt had been making me sick.

Despite enduring these additional significant trials and feeling the emotions that come with them, I found that something within me had been permanently shifted. I discovered a newfound steadfastness in my faith and strength. Rather than succumbing to despair and fear, I had chosen to lean on trust and the notion that certain events are predetermined. This prevented my anxiety from spiraling out of control and anchored me when I felt myself coming undone. I kept my eyes fixed on God, my lighthouse amidst the stormy seas, trusting to be guided back to safety as I had before. Through it all, I understood that while life events such as these can really test us, they also possess a transformative power—they protect, permit, and propel us forward.

It didn't happen overnight. As you have read, multiple events led to trust becoming my 'emergence.' It might not be the same for you, but with only one life to live, I encourage you to embark on a reflective journey through the highs and lows you've faced. Discern those moments where divine intervention may have played a role, whether unfolding gently or charging in full steam ahead. Envision how things might have been different if it never took place. Take a deep breath, trust, and witness the transformation. It's time to let go; don't allow the unknown to control you any longer. After all, life is predominantly beyond our control, so why waste another moment in debilitating pain, fear, anxiety, or depression? Hand it over, release it.

Let FAITH and TRUST stand as unwavering pillars, allow them to bear the weight of our struggles, and offer the promise of healing and liberation, signifying the journey through life's trials and tribulations, a testament to the indomitable human spirit emerging whole and resilient.

About Amie Solomon

Amie Solomon, a beacon of strength and resilience, has traversed a diverse career path. From her roots as a seasoned corporate marketing professional, she transitioned into a TV personality and wildlife advocate, all while maintaining her primary love for writing.

As a fiction and nonfiction Author, she skillfully crafts narratives that ignite imagination to inspire and empower, enlightening and inviting readers into worlds where possibilities abound.

Driven by a profound mission, Amie serves as a compassionate guide for grieving parents, drawing from her own experiences of loss, including the birthing of her daughter Lola without breath and recurrent miscarriages. Through her writing, she illuminates paths of love and hope amid darkness, offering solace to those in similar struggles.

Her journey has garnered widespread media recognition, with her stories of baby loss and miscarriage featured across various editorials, social platforms, and a prominent Australian television channel.

Beyond her literary endeavors, Amie embraces the delightful chaos of motherhood, crafting literacy magic amidst the hustle of dodging Legos and sticky fingers.

In every word written and shared, Amie Solomon embodies resilience, empathy, and the transformative power of storytelling.

You can find and connect with Amie at Website: www.authorajane.com or Instagram: @amiejanesolomon

Great Expectations

By Anna Dawson

Introduction

Great expectations; the title of the Charles Dickens classic is not a book for me. It's the realization that I've had expectations about many things without being aware of them. Expectations about my life, the way the people in my life would behave, and even how I thought God should act. I realize now that I owe God and others, including myself, an apology for these one-sided agreements that I thought were concretely in place. One of the biggest things I didn't expect to face was the chaos and carnage I did with my daughter and stepson in their teenage years, especially given my profession. But I did, and for the past four years, I've been walking this earth, venturing from one monumental low to another and facing one shattered expectation after another.

Surrendering to the reality of my life has taken me far from where I expected to be, but at the same time, it feels as though I'm on the path to which I belong; A path where I get to share my personal experiences of parenting teenagers who were at times their greatest threat to their own lives. I've been amazed at how I've been able to do this, not only alcohol-free but with a continuous dose of gratitude and awe. Like the awe of the lotus flower that blooms from the muddiest depths of my life to remind me how beautiful and precious life still is in the dark.

Low Point

I first met death when I was five years old when my infant brother died from Sudden Infant Death Syndrome (SIDS). I met death again when I was 12, when my father committed suicide. I've few memories of my brother and father, yet they've remained with me and are present throughout my life. Their impact prompted me to do things differently when my children were infants and teenagers to avoid more SIDS and suicidal deaths. So when my then 14-year-old daughter attempted suicide, I went into shock. In the early hours of the 9th of March, 2020, my daughter, who couldn't stop vomiting, told me and her stepfather that she'd swallowed a box of Panadol to try and kill herself. My world was spinning by the time we arrived at the hospital. How could I have not seen this? As her mother and as a child protection professional? It wasn't long before we were ushered from the hospital waiting room to an emergency bed. She was given anti-vomiting treatment after anti-vomiting treatment, and yet it continued. With no food left in her stomach, she was just hurling up bile. Bright, fluro yellow, thick bile continuously emerging from her mouth and nose. Tears fell from her face because of the pain and agony of the incessant onslaught of her body purging.

She was soon moved to the Paediatric ward, which was good because they let parents stay overnight. I wasn't going anywhere. And I didn't, except for the two hours my son stayed with her while I went home to get clothes. I showered, ate, and slept at the hospital. At some point, a doctor scared me when he casually announced that she would need 24 hours of hourly antibodies given to her intravenously. Afterward, further testing was required to see if she had permanent damage to her kidneys and, if so, could need a kidney transplant. So, we waited. I pushed the recliner chair as close to her hospital bed as I could. We were head to toe, side by side, and I held her hand all night long as we tried to sleep through the night with the nurses coming in every hour to do their checks. Time seemed to slow right down, and all I could do was concentrate on caring for my daughter and try not to get bogged down by the guilt, shame, and regret that was chasing me. This was the lowest point in my adult life so far. I didn't want to meet death again, especially not with my own child. Please, God, anything but that.

High Point / Low Point

Fast forward three years, and my daughter was healthy and happy. We were getting along so great that we started planning and saving for a three-week-long Europe trip, beginning and ending in Paris. Before departing in late 2023, I'd been adamant this trip would be one in which our relationship as mother and daughter would become even closer than we'd become over the past few years. I anticipated it would be like a celebration of all the hurdles and obstacles we'd faced and overcome in recent times. My daughter and I became close, but not as I had expected.

We arrived in Paris around lunchtime on a hot October day and went to our hotel, which was within walking distance of the Eiffel Tower. We spent the afternoon and early evening exploring the city before walking back to our hotel room for the night, ready for the adventure to start.

But before I could get out of bed in the morning, I received a phone call from my brother-in-law and met death again. My stepson had died. By my calculations, he died roughly around the time we'd landed in Paris. I screamed and screamed. My daughter lay beside me, witnessing my reaction.

I briefly spoke to my husband, but he didn't make sense. I could hear the shock in his voice. Immediately after the call, we started our trip back home to Australia. Instead of going on a dream holiday with my daughter, I was now facing my worst fear: losing a child. My only stepchild. I wondered if I would've made it home without my daughter. After four flight delays and finally a cancellation, I had a panic attack at the Paris airport. Attendants were trying to take me to the hospital. While I was unable to breathe, my tiny yet powerful daughter hounded airport staff face-to-face and by phone, reiterating that I was not going to the hospital. Nothing was going to make a grieving mother better by going to the hospital at that moment, and I just needed to get home.

When I arrived home four days later, my husband didn't have the strength to go on the drive to pick me up from the airport. When I saw him for the first time, he was in his shed in the backyard, and when he saw me, he started to crumble. He walked halfway and fell on the floor in front of me. I met him on the floor, and we stayed in each other's arms. God only knows how long. Sensing friends watching us cry and crying themselves. I could no longer live in 'this isn't happening land.' There was a childless father in front of me, and I had lost my one and only stepchild. The week was a blur, with the funeral, wake, and never-ending procession of visitors. There was an incredible amount of alcohol consumed around this time, but not by me, as I had been alcohol-free since 2020.

Quitting Alcohol

My mother told me from a young age that alcoholism ran in our family and that my grandmother had died at age 50 from Cirrhosis of the liver. Subliminally, my mother also communicated that if we were 'happy-go-lucky' drinkers, it wasn't a problem. I never questioned my drinking based on my family's drinking rules. I never needed to. I was always within the parameters of what I thought my family defined as acceptable drinking. But there came a time when I started to educate myself on alcohol because I began to suspect I had a problem.

Towards the end of my drinking days, my first main motivation for giving up alcohol was my stepson. In his last year of school, at age 17, he went out one night with some of his newly licensed school friends, and one would not return to their family due to a motorbike crash. This was the final catalyst for my stepson's descent into a world of addiction and self-harm. Over the next five years, he would leave a trail of destruction that would ultimately lead to his life ending when he was 22 years of age. At the start, I looked around my stepson's life and saw no one in his life was sober, including me. No one could provide a sober example of how to live life in pain, on life's terms, and be able to ride life's highs and lows without substances. I recognized it was hypocritical of me and other adults in his life to point the finger at him and tell him to stop doing something they were not willing to do. So, in 2019, I stopped lecturing and quit alcohol. It wasn't as easy as I thought and only lasted fifty-four days. I got the motivation to try again ten months later after my daughter's suicide attempt. This time, I got help and have recently celebrated four years alcohol-free.

I realized soon after quitting alcohol that I attempted to control something when my world felt so out of control. Knowing this now, I still choose to be alcohol-free. I've come to accept I can't control people's lives, including their addictions, but I can influence people, and I can choose whether that influence is positive or negative. It breaks my heart that my stepson didn't find recovery. But it warms my heart that I've still managed to be a positive influence in my family. Both my children are alcohol and drug-free, and a sibling diagnosed with stage one Cirrhosis of the liver is now in recovery from alcohol as well.

Expectations

In the early days of my recovery from alcohol, I heard the saying, '*Expectations breed resentment*' (unknown). It stayed with me and illuminated that I had many expectations, from mundane to more fanciful ones, but most hid under my radar as unconscious expectations. At first, I struggled to recognize these expectations, but my first major uncovering came when I realized that I unconsciously thought God understood He could take my father but not my children. So, when my daughter attempted suicide, I went into shock. I spent days when she wasn't around sitting on my couch, staring out into space, only managing to do the basics. Slowly, I started to recognize more expectations. Next were my expectations about the clothes I thought my daughter should wear. I was mortified at her Adidas and Nike clothes, TN shoes, and straightened curly hair. No. I expected her to dress in a beautiful boho style with gorgeous, long, curly hair. Highlighting her beautiful hair in a way I never got to.

Then, she didn't look like she was going to finish high school like I thought she was going to. I'd always sensed one of my children would finish high school and one wouldn't, but I thought her older brother wouldn't make it because of how challenging school was for him. On the other hand, my daughter breezed through primary school, but within 18 months of starting high school, she'd gone from nearly a perfect child in primary school to a girl that I barely recognized. I started getting called to the school for crimes more heinous than her brother had committed, let alone the out-of-school petty crimes and misdemeanors.

Slowly, I put down my expectations of my daughter and started concentrating on her strengths, talents, and the dreams she had for her own life. Fast forward four years, and despite not finishing high school, she is an incredibly independent, industrious, and spiritual young woman. She moved interstate by herself and is in a stable relationship, home, and job with an internationally known airline, but most importantly, she is happy and healthy. I'm incredibly proud of her and of myself for the effort I put into changing so that I could be the mother she needed rather than the one I wanted to be.

Conclusion

My life has not looked like I thought it would in the last few years. After my daughter's suicide attempt, I quit alcohol and started to face my life and expectations head-on. Since this time, I've seen my daughter recover from substance misuse and poor mental health, and I've seen my stepson die from the very same enemies. There are so many things I don't understand. I don't know why my daughter found recovery and my stepson died so early in his life, on the very day my daughter and I started our dream Europe trip together. I've faced my worst fear, losing a child, though albeit a stepchild, he was my stepson for eight years, and I loved him dearly.

What's interesting about the book Great Expectations is that the author, Charles Dickens, was persuaded to rewrite a happier ending to the original version he wrote. I cannot rewrite what has happened in my life, but I can make positive choices about how I think about the past and what I will do in the future - choices that can uplift not only my hurting self but others I already know or those I meet along this sometimes harsh but always precious gift called life.

About Anna Dawson

Anna Dawson combines her passion for supporting children, young people, and families as a registered Social Worker with her professional and personal experiences of calamities and worst-case scenarios. She attributes these experiences and her personality traits to her vast capacity to hold space for families in the depths and provide ongoing hope and support.

As a Child Safety Officer for the Queensland State Government, Anna has the perfect mix of academic success and front-line work experience. She completed a child protection-themed honors thesis in her undergraduate Social Work degree and graduated from university with First Class Honours and an academic medal for her coursework. She has worked in the broad area of child protection since 2010 in various roles across the northern and southern regions of Queensland, giving her an in-depth look at the Queensland child protection system within both government and non-government agencies.

Anna is the mother of an adult son and daughter and stepmother to an adult stepson. She knows firsthand, from professional and personal experience, how difficult it can be to raise children and young people who struggle with mental health and addiction. She and her husband supported their three children as they individually struggled with a range of issues, including mental health and substances. Her stepson passed away in 2023, at age 22, from his ongoing battle with mental health and substances. This, along with her diagnoses of several chronic illnesses since 2020, has been the cataclysm for her to start transitioning from her current government role to a yet undetermined, fresh, and healing venture. The starting point is sharing some of her personal experiences in the collaborative book 'Emergence' by Mosaic Media.

Since losing her stepson, Anna's calling to help families not feel isolated and find some peace during difficult times has intensified rather than diminished. She's more passionate than ever about finding flexible, accessible, and innovative ways to deliver quality mental health support to children, young people, and their families in the ever-changing Australian landscape.

Anna lives with her husband, son, cat, and two cheeky labradors on the land of the Kabi Kabi people, the seaside suburb of Redcliffe, Queensland, Australia. She is also a foster carer for Labrador Retriever Rescue Australia, and it's not uncommon for her to have another friendly wagging tail at her home.

You can connect with Anna at Email Anna.Dawson@pinklotusfamilysupport.com.au or Instagram: @Pink_Lotus_Family_Support

Marble

By Carmel Charlesworth

Emergence – Latin root *Emergere* - *Bring to Light*

"The treatment is working so well," he said while studying my most recent scans, "we'll continue with another round."

Perfect. Great news.

You would think that to be a positive thing. The best news you could hope for. And it is, in every sense of the medical profession, it can't get any better than that, except when that's not the conversation you had built up in your head from twelve months prior and had been working with to get you through to this point where it would all be normal again. It's an interesting concept, the way our minds work. Gathering information from multiple sources, including ourselves, and formulating how a scenario will play out in real life. No matter how much you strive to avoid the unknown, it's always present. Looming in the background are the shadows of doubt, waiting until the eleventh hour to appear in our plans—the so-called *spanner in the works*. When the new scenario is laid out in front of us with the extra tool playing a massive part we didn't anticipate, the real challenge is to pick up that tool and allow it to stay, whether wanted or not.

The new year arrives, goals are made, and intentions set. People say I want the old me back - more vibrant, happier, skinnier, youthful. The version of ourselves is perceived as *better* in our minds for many different reasons. The plan is implemented with a new routine or different way of doing things to obtain our past selves. We strive to reach the memory we have from that time. Most of us have done this at some point, me included, several times over. We look back at the people we used to be and fantasize that we can be them in the present, so we set our minds to becoming them again. Rarely do we acknowledge that our past selves served a purpose and created the platform for who we are now, but ultimately, we can never be them again. The ghosts of our pasts haunt us and push us to feel guilty over a natural evolution of self, yet it doesn't have to be this way if we don't allow it to dictate our present.

I often think of the version of me in early 2021. I was celebrating and blissfully unaware that my world would change in a way I could never have prepared for. I was searching for answers to a question I didn't really want to ask. My fingers, feet, and torso numb with altered sensation. Darkness in the form of a headache that never left me. A level of fatigue that no amount of rest or sleep could alleviate. Mental fog so thick it left me struggling to remember words during conversations. All symptoms that, after months of testing, gave rise to my new normal: life with a Multiple Sclerosis diagnosis. As I move through this revelation and the emotions that flow with it, I try to make sense of it all, to explain how this actually feels—a tangible way of expressing this betrayal. I see a young girl with a collection of marbles, each one she's named and knows individually. The color, the feel, the size, the weight, and the way each one could be used and played with. She is comfortable with how they fit together in the collection and work with each other to complete her set. One day, a word in the form of a whisper sweeps through, takes them away, and replaces them with a new bag of marbles. She opens up the bag, and the marbles are completely different. She takes them out and studies them individually, unsure of where they fit within the collection.

Re-learning how they feel to her and how to use them. Her sadness overshadows the opportunity she's been given, and her perspective on the gift is not about possibility and hope but grief and loss for her old set. Marble is viewed as a stone of potential, awaiting a master carver's touch. Its distinctive veins and swirls from mineral deposits in the stone react to the heat and pressure in unique ways. My search for Self and how my body works now is dark within that bag. The parts of me I knew no longer feel the same way. My reaction to the heat and pressure of the situation is new to me, but perhaps not a unique experience after a significant medical condition is revealed. Hidden beyond the surface for only me to see are my distinctive veins and swirls. The newly formed pattern fused deep within cannot be measured or viewed by another. I am both the stone and the master carver intertwined as one.

My specialist divulged that his day leading up to our appointment hadn't been particularly positive, but my results were excellent, and I was amazing. Amazing. Amazing, it didn't feel like that word should roll off your tongue and be spoken to another person. I didn't think at that moment that I had done anything to deserve that praise. All I heard was my treatment was to continue beyond what I had believed was the end, and I watched the goalposts move before my eyes. My brain wasn't ready for that next step. I thought this was it. It turns out I was wrong. So, the spanner in the works begins to take shape, rearranging the picture in my head with how the next chapter of my life looks. A wave of grief crashes through me while in my mind, I begin crossing out the things in my life I was going to do, pulling apart the vision of what the next stage was going to be—the new, new me. I thought I'd done this already and accepted the new version of myself. Yet here I am. Again.

The start of my MS journey allowed me to really see my life from a new perspective. The what-ifs and uncertainties forced me to focus on the joys I had in my life and what no longer served me. I cleared the way to connect with what was important and what I truly wanted. Nothing like a massive health revelation to put you on your ass and click its fingers in your face. Have I got your attention now? I felt the shock waves of that declaration in every fiber of my being. It forced me to do the work. The hard, ugly work that leaves you open and vulnerable as you chip away at yourself from all angles. I left a comfortable and secure job of 16 years because I was unfulfilled to pursue the role I wanted. I resigned from my position as a Tae Kwon Do instructor; my balance and ability to teach and remember techniques weren't at the standard I wanted for myself or exposed to others. I reigned in the areas of my life that weren't absolutely necessary to create pockets of space for me to heal and rest. All with an end date in mind. Once treatment is finished in twelve months I can pick up where I left off in a blaze of glory of what I had overcome. Through my shedding of self, I see now that Carmel is gone. The version of me who devoted so much time to perfecting these things and to putting others first is simply no longer here. As the layers unravel, they reveal a blessing in the form of a grief messenger. Nowhere to hide. No way to avoid the process. Only through to the other side of me.

As I research what best practices for those diagnosed with MS are, I find a lot of information covering well-being - what an individual can do to slow the progression of the MS symptoms. Diet, exercise, mental health, cognitive tools; the list is expansive. And for someone as new to this as me, I've struggled. Who am I? I've turned the page on my previous self and am left with this woman staring back at me in the mirror, who I no longer recognize. I have all these emotions surrounding the duality of this person, and I don't know where to start. I'm scared to try, fearing not achieving the old me goals. I'm afraid to push her and go too far with those body boundaries. What will happen if I do? MS is a tricky disease. The symptoms can come and go, or they can stay permanently. Things you do or don't do can make them worse. It's an uncharted road of trial and error. With my body determining long periods of strenuous activity as a symptom aggravator, Yoga and stretching is where I begin. Gentle movements and moments of calm and clarity to become present with myself. Despite how it may appear – it's far from easy. Fortunately, I have my own space to do such sessions, and I often retreat here to recharge.

I commence the beginner's episode on my subscribed channel and start well. I can stretch, bend my leg, breathe into my belly, and clear my mind. Plank. Hold. Plank to downward dog. Hold. The numbness in my fingers makes this extremely uncomfortable. My arms weakened from the time away from regular training and Tae Kwon Do conditioning. I last ten seconds before I succumb to my body's protests and crash down to the mat. I try again with the same heartbreaking result. I cry. Frustrated. Defeated. It shouldn't be this hard. I've done harder things before. What's wrong with me? Nothing and everything. At that moment, I realized my past benchmarks no longer existed. I have no standard of what I'm expected to do. The new me is here, and she is here to stay. I look at my reflection in the mirror, "So you better figure out what the fuck you are going to do because crying on a Yoga mat is not it."

What do I want to do with the new version of myself? Acknowledge her. Allow her. Accept her. Adore her—all the things I haven't been doing for the last six months. I created an enemy of myself with misguided anger. She didn't deserve my anger. She's been here waiting to become me, and I've held her at arm's length, not allowing her to step into my soul and skin for fear she wouldn't be enough. I'm scared she won't be enough. But here's the real pearl of wisdom that forty years of life and an MS diagnosis have given me. Whatever version of yourself you have right now, that version is here to serve you. Not hurt you, not hold you back, or to lay blame on. How you choose to serve yourself is the version you will create in the now. Be of service to yourself.

My story is a coming-of-age story. The mirror moments that carve our creation. I understand now I don't have a disability or limitations; I have boundaries. Body Boundaries. A different type than we're accustomed to hearing about, with personal, relationship, and physical boundaries that have already made a stand, but body boundaries we discover, put in place, and test after a new version of ourselves appears. What am I now capable of? I owe it to my new self to learn. Shedding is the new stage of grief and healing combined. One cannot exist without the other. Not only is healing not linear, but it's building, redesigning, and carving all at once. We are masterpieces of our lives. The perfect creation, ever-evolving. There are no instructions on how to be you, so why do you think you've got it wrong? You haven't. You've been divinely orchestrated the whole time. Embrace your divinity: past, present, and future.

About Carmel Charlesworth

Carmel is an authenticity advocate who creates a safe space for others to explore the truth of their hearts. Through her understanding of the evolving self and personal transformation, she is passionate about body boundaries. She empowers and guides others to overcome fear and judgment to find their inner beauty and authentic self.

Devoting her time to the community, Carmel serves as a Justice of The Peace and an NRL sports Trainer. Her love for assisting people shows in the embodiment of her core values of compassion, love, and empathy.

Carmel's literary prowess is evident in her international bestselling co-authorship of 'Extraordinary—Inspiring Stories of Living and Loving Beyond the Label '. Writing is Carmel's healing modality of choice, creating a foundation for finding a calming inner strength. She continues to inspire and motivate others through her writing, as a public speaker, and as a passionate MS Ambassador.

She has been featured in various media, including MS Australia Podcast The Raw Nerve, Living in Logan magazine, Logan West News, and Brisbane Catholic Education.

Carmel lives with her husband, who she describes as her rock and soul mate, in Brisbane, where they raise their two sons.

Connect with Carmel on Facebook- Carmel Charlesworth Author

The Softening

By Debra Nathanson

Curled under my desk in the fetal position was not how I thought I'd expect life to be with a career as a psychotherapist working with Veterans, nearing my 40th birthday, and planning a wedding to marry my boyfriend of nine years.

A nervous breakdown wasn't the vision I had planned or worked so hard for. I thought that helping others who were suffering was my role here on earth—the Hero, the Savior, the wounded healer.

Perhaps I had a hidden wish that if I saw others transmute and transform their trauma and pains, it would somehow heal mine by penetrating slowly into the deeper layers of my being that I had covered up for so long. Why would I want to go digging into my past and do more trauma work on myself when, at the time, the life I thought I was living was going pretty well? In fact, it was some of the smoothest times in my life.

I had 15 years of sobriety under my belt, a postgraduate degree, and solid employment, and I was ready to marry the man I loved. I was a homeowner and a badass female Harley rider who could keep up with some of the most notorious and toughest "bikers" in the world. I had a full social community and groups of friends and was loved by my family. Some would say I had it all going on for me. A successful therapist who also sponsored, mentored, and helped other women find their courage and independence both in recovery and riding motorcycles. Sharing the spark of Life, the ride, and ultimate freedom. My ego filled my cup well, and it kept me fueled daily. I was like a machine, constantly on the go with a drive to help heal others, either in a therapy office or on two wheels.

I had a caseload of over 300 clients at one time (most had severe trauma and were disabled with PTSD). Here I was, thinking I had it all together, when all of a sudden, my mental health crumbled and blasted my past wide open. I had been completely numb to my internal self, playing the Hero, helping save lives during the weekday, and riding, playing, and rolling hard in my personal life. I ignored my higher self screaming at me. My body constantly tried to slow me down in a plea for attention. I found I could keep functioning as a machine as long as I stayed on the cocktail mix of prescription pills that the doctors gave me to hush all the symptoms. I was checked out and allowed the medical world to have power over me; I became an energetic rag doll being thrown around the world.

The cover-ups I created could only go on for so long until I was found hiding under my desk that day, trembling, feeling myself scream- WHY NOW? I could no longer hide. I finally found the mirrors that cleared my denial and numbness while facilitating a military sexual trauma group. I saw myself in the ladies I was helping; that's when my past violent traumas popped out of hiding, and judgment and comparison stepped in. After clearing the group quickly, I broke harder than I thought I ever could. I felt something in my brain. It had an internal sound that made my entire being jump, jump to attention through fear, fear that I had really done it now. I had finally pushed the limits of my consciousness, and my brain had snapped like a rubber band. Pandora's box had begun to unravel, and it was clear I had to finally face my own past. My co-workers called my soon-to-be husband and permitted him to enter the military base where I worked, and he pried me out from under my desk and took me home in a sedated state.

Nothing felt safe anymore. I thought I had been so tough. My neighborhood was tough; my friends and the communities I ran with were tough. I had some of the toughest clients, and my life was tough. I had always been tough! And now I found myself broken. My psychiatrist placed me on immediate disability and wanted me to go to an inpatient ward. After assuring him I had no desire to harm myself, I was able to stay home, where I was bedridden and heavily sedated in my room, clutched to my dogs, or frantically ripping at my garden. When I regained my strength, I turned to my old, comfortable friend, my Harley. Twisting that throttle was the only true place I felt I had control over. I could control my speed, yet most times, I could hardly do that. My bike was the only place I truly felt alive because it was the closest to death I could get; I tasted life and death in the wind, in all my senses, pushing me harder to play, tease, and taunt death while begging myself to stay alive. I also have had great respect for Death. It had been almost 20 years since my first fiance was killed on our bike. It was my way of grieving and has become my greatest teacher. On my bike, my senses were full throttle as well, and it was where I could touch the edges of life and connect with those who had passed beyond the veil. Riding my motorcycle was emotional and spiritual maintenance; it got me through just about everything these past 30 years. It was a place I knew, somewhere I could go on autopilot and let the breeze take my worries and be free.

One would think I was at peace on the outside with as many miles riding as I had under me, yet here I was, emotionally bleeding out, depressed, and on the verge of psychosis. My stories flooded out of my mouth to anyone who would listen, often purging old traumas, old pains, others' traumas, and others' pains. I had become the epitome of the "wounded healer" and the "poster child" for complex PTSD exacerbated by work-related compassion fatigue and indoor air environments. After all, I had received an official stamp from the government, I had been granted early retirement disability from the Veterans Administration and Social Security disability for Complex PTSD (and) "hypersensitivity to indoor and outdoor environments due to Toxic Mold," whoa that was a mouthful, and it was a lot to digest. It was now Official; I was Messed Up. I had been given a disability label and got paid to be sick. It has been over 15 years since I've been stamped "unable to have full-time gainful employment."

I play(ed) the sick role well, and yes, every once in a while, the little sick girl still wants to come out, reminding me of the ways I play the victim role: the broken, damaged, and darkened one, and one I've learned to tame. I've made choices that I'm not so proud of throughout my life, where I've carried deep shame, as many of us do. The awareness and recognition of the Victim, Villian, and Hero roles have been one of the biggest and ongoing shifts in my continued softening.

After marrying my partner of nine years, we divorced only 18 months later. I chose to leave him abruptly; I chose change. I couldn't keep going like this. I just could not sustain the life I was living anymore. Even though, up to this point, it was one of the few times where it was the calm in my life, it just wasn't working anymore.

I was bored and numb, popping prescription pills and smoking a lot of cannabis, gardening at home, and riding my motorcycle whenever and wherever I wanted. Leaving my husband was a soul calling I had to follow, no matter the pain I caused others. I had to break away from the life I had created; quick shifts were a pattern in my life, and I did it again.

I had often felt different and somewhat "cursed," and it was not unlike me to blame karma and the "spiritual world" and make 'It' responsible for the outcome of my choices and my current situation. A local psychic guided me to help lift the current "curse." This was the doorway where I began my softening and spiritual journey to my heart, soul, and Oneness. It wasn't a "return to love" for me, as that was a hard reality to choke down. I only had flickers and memories of what love and self-love tasted and felt like before, yet they were never fully expressed. I've collected those hardened and broken fractals of my life that I've tossed all over the place and brought them into my heart.

While it wasn't the smoothest process, it started with a brutal cold turkey detox of eight different prescription pills. (Vicodin, Lexapro, Adderall, Cymbalta, Xanax, and Soma, to name just a few) with the help of a good dose of food poisoning and my incredible support team, my new boyfriend Bob and my best friend and sponsor Angie; both had moved in and helped me to get through it, regain my strength, and thus, began the process and new goal of shifting a lifelong mind of hard pessimism to a more positive mind.

It's been over eight years now since I was on prescription meds and a full-blown pessimist. That shift didn't come easy, as nothing does for this kind of freedom: freedom from addictions, dependency, and emotional and mental decline, which I've been very intimate with during this painful process of shape-shifting and becoming softer. It was time to embrace my hard life, love it, and finally let it go.

Once I found the Will to Live and Love myself, the healing began to set in with my partner's and my friends' help and continuous support. I became hungry and desperate for life, answers, guidance, and positivity. I attended weekly in-person meditation classes and learned countless techniques and tools to help calm me and clear negative energy. I was introduced to and trained in the law of attraction, Kundalini yoga, plant medicine, energy and breathwork, and sound healing. This blossomed into more intensive shifts of learning, remembering, honoring, and embracing the multi-dimensional self and the various realities, finally allowing me to see all living things connected as one. I was no longer separated or hard; I began to feel a connection and a new sense of love and softening in my heart.

My eyes and visions became clearer, my years of night terrors diminished, and I was excited about what was coming and what I was creating. And create I did. Going back to work and being a therapist wasn't what was on my agenda. I was done with my story and everyone else's story. I was talked out and done listening. I started to attune and pay more attention to myself and my environment. I began a small home crafting medicinal cannabis product line of tincture and salves for pets and people that was rewarding and allowed me to continue to help others. I also co-created large motorcycle events with the intention of creating a non-profit for injured riders. I felt on top of the world as the event became known worldwide. After seven years of increased success with the event, it came crashing down hard and abruptly. It had been stolen and consumed by greed and lust for money by one of the main sponsors. A legal gag order was placed on me, and I was demoralized on social media and haunted in my mind by the thieves; I no longer felt safe once again. I was unable to speak my truth and began to lose my passion. The new spiritual shifts I was creating did not allow me to play with the community I had moved freely around and in for decades. Everything started to feel different, and I could not unsee the ugly that lived there. I felt a change coming, and it came quickly.

My father had a massive stroke and lost his ability to speak and function. I moved to be by his side and help care for him for the short seven weeks he stayed alive. My dad was my lifelong "hero," my reason to not give up on life, no matter how hard I wanted to. He was the reason I kept pushing forward. He was the reason I originally got sober; he had rescued me off the streets and pulled the needle out of my arm. He was the reason I kept my motorcycle upright and gave me a reason to live, strive to be better, be honest, and, most of all, be happy. As he exhaled, I inhaled his love and happiness of life into me. I now had no choice but to learn to live for myself, be awake, and no longer numb out and hide.

Since I still had little to no control of my throttle hand or passion left when I rode my Harley, and being in deep grief while riding can make for a bad mix. The kickstand had to come down; it was time to stop chasing asphalt (death) and go within, stop running and drop deeper into my heart and my body, and start doing some more excavating, begin working and applying the healing tools I was learning.

As I write this, even my best friend and riding sister Angela transcended with an unexpected twist of her throttle only a few months back, another reminder of the thin line I chose to dance on. I dedicate this chapter to her in honor of her helping me to retrain my brain with optimism, hope, and love. I also dedicate this to all those who have gone before me, those who will come after me, and those who are currently with me. This Breath, we breathe together now as One.

The journey to my heart has been a long road of over 50 years to finally quiet my negative mind chatter enough to hear the beats of love and gratitude come through. Deep down, I knew that this hardened and stubborn girl needed many trials and hurdles to slam into again and again until surrendering was the only thing left to do.

I have returned to helping others. I have a small private practice now and show up for offerings to anyone who presents themselves. I have also begun to ride my motorcycle again, reuniting with a new attitude of mindfulness and respect. I keep a daily meditation practice along with a well-stocked toolbox that allows me to dance as a multidimensional being where joy and suffering coexist while continuously softening and expanding my heart. I am complete today, just as I AM.

About Debra Nathanson

Debra is the creator of Magical Healings and Sacred Psychotherapy. With over 35 years as a licensed clinical social worker and psychotherapist, plus decades of Shamanic training and personal lived experiences, she guides those seeking an authentic, heart-centered life.

With a warm, integrative and eclectic approach to helping others, Debra plays within the multi-dimensional fields, working with various energies, embracing the dark shadows while walking the path of light.

As a wisdom keeper, Debra holds many qualifications that serve multiple situations, from the lower to the higher functioning and from crisis to the calm. A few of her specialties include working with complex and severe trauma, death and grief, combat veterans, addictions, and mood and nervous system dysregulation. She is certified in plant medicine guidance and integration, Kundalini Yoga, meditation, clairvoyance, sound healing, and sacred rose medicine.

Currently residing outside of Austin, Texas, with her beloved husband and their dog "Nugget," they are often out adventuring in their RV across the country, either soaking up some magical waters or riding their Harleys or UTV through the back country roads.

You can find and connect with Debra at Website: www.magicalhealings.company.site

Through the Echoes of Time

By Elle Embers

For as long as I can remember, I've always felt like an outsider, a misfit, a solitary figure navigating a world that never quite felt like home. It was almost as though I had been plucked from another time, another place, and thrust into a world that clashed with the whispers of my very soul. I found it frustrating that while others found themselves vibrantly navigating this modern life, I found myself adrift, tethered to a past I couldn't fully grasp, and I feared I never would.

As a child, I was always a bit wiser and more in tune with the world than most, almost as though I'd been here before. Like, I'd played this game, and I knew the rules. People often called me an 'old soul,' but the term never quite captured the weight of the disconnection I truly felt from those around me. I felt like an outcast, a puzzle piece from a different era, trying desperately to fit into a picture that was not my own, a picture I struggled to even comprehend. Most of my childhood carried this strange sense of déjà vu, as if I wasn't experiencing it for the first time but as if I were reliving moments from a past life. Each was a jarring reminder of my disconnection to this modern time and place. It was as if I were caught in a perpetual loop; places, people, and experiences all seemed to spark a sense of recollection, like I was reliving moments from a life I couldn't quite remember. And yet, amidst the confusion, there was this strange sense of familiarity, safety, a whisper of recognition that left me longing for something that felt just out of reach.

My unexplainable connection to the spirit world only seemed to deepen the divide between myself and those around me. While others recoiled at the mention of ghosts and spirits, I found solace in the unseen realms, a refuge from the harsh realities of this mismatched life. But connecting with my spirit team, ancestors, and other entities came with its own hurdles.

Navigating the world of spirits was like trying to find your way in a crowded room where everyone speaks a different language. Each spirit, whether a guide from my spirit team or an ancestor, had its own unique way of communicating. It was either a mix of words, sounds, signs, feelings, and energies that often left me feeling like I was missing the punchline of an inside joke. Without a mentor to show me the ropes, I stumbled through this maze of communication, sometimes taking steps in the wrong direction before finding my footing again. It was a journey of trial and error, of learning through experience rather than instruction, and just hoping that, eventually, I'd be able to make sense of it all.

But amidst the frustration, there was a sense of wonder, a feeling that I was part of something bigger than myself despite the language barriers and the uncertainty. In those moments of connection, I felt a commonality with the spirits; maybe we were all just looking for a place to feel like we belonged? No matter the time, place, or dimension. But with each attempt to share my spiritual experiences with those around me, I felt the rift between myself and others widen, leaving me to navigate the divide alone, separating me further from this modern world that I longed to be a part of.

I yearned for a time and place that felt like home, where my abilities would be embraced rather than feared. My dreams were constantly filled with visions of spirits and messages, distant lands, and bygone eras, each one feeling more like a memory than a figment of my imagination. Perhaps I was recalling echoes from another existence, but if so, what was the purpose of it all?

Then came the devastating loss of my mother, a loss that shattered my fragile sense of belonging and thrust me into a world of grief and uncertainty as I headed into my teenage years. In the wake of her passing, my connection to the spirit world intensified, blurring the boundaries between the living and the dead. I was consumed by a new sense of fear I couldn't name, a fear of the unknown that lurked just beyond the veil. As grief deepened my connection to the spirit world, I grappled with this newfound fear of my abilities, desperate to shield myself from the overwhelming flood of emotions that threatened to consume me. When death claimed another loved one in my early twenties, it was as if the ground crumbled beneath me, leaving me to grapple with the void left in its wake.

I struggled to make sense of the senseless, to find meaning in a world filled with pain and loss. It was in those dark moments that I began to question everything I thought I knew about life and death; searching for answers in the depths of my very own soul, I embarked on a journey of self-discovery, determined to unravel the mysteries of my existence and the forces that shaped it. It was during this search for answers that I stumbled upon past life regression therapy. A form of soul therapy that allows us to access memories stored away in our subconscious mind from previous incarnations that may influence our current thoughts, emotions, or behaviors.

Through these guided sessions, I delved into the depths of my subconscious mind, unraveling the threads of past lives woven into the fabric of my soul. Each regression revealed glimpses of a different world and time that felt strangely familiar yet achingly distant. Through the haze of memory and emotion, I revisited these past lifetimes, each sharing a revelation, a piece of the puzzle that was my soul's journey through time. Through these experiences, I came to understand that my relationship with time was unlike that of others, and as I delved deeper, I discovered a truth that shook me to my very core. This truth explained the gnawing sense of displacement that had plagued me my entire life.

I discovered that a part of my soul had remained tethered to another time, from a sacrifice made in a moment of selfless love that left a void that echoed through the ages.

With this newfound knowledge came a sense of purpose, a determination to reclaim what was rightfully mine and forge a new path toward healing and wholeness in this lifetime. So, I embarked on a journey unlike any other, guided by the whispers of the past and the promise of a brighter future.

The road to healing was full of challenges, each a test of my strength and resilience. Yet, through it all, I persevered, fuelled by a stubborn refusal to be defined by my past or bound by the limitations of it. I was done feeling like an outcast, like a visitor in my own life, and I was ready to reclaim my sense of unity, belonging, and home.

And then, one day, it happened.

It was a moment of reckoning, a convergence of past and present that left me breathless with wonder. A moment in time where the threads of my past could be rewoven, the narrative of a bygone era could be rewritten, and the fragments of my soul scattered across lifetimes could finally find their way home to me.

It was then that I realized that time was never meant to be my captor; it was not a prison to be escaped, but rather a guide of inspiration, leading me through the tapestry of my life, weaving together moments of joy, sorrow, and everything in between. In the fluidity of time, we find the freedom to explore, create, dream, and embrace each passing moment as a gift, a precious opportunity to write our own story upon the canvas of eternity.

As I stood on the threshold of my transformation, I felt a surge of energy course through my veins, a rush of power, unlike anything I had ever known. As I embodied this newfound knowledge and strength, I knew that my journey was far from over and that the best was yet to come.

Armed with this newfound understanding of myself and my abilities, I embraced my connection to the spirit world with open arms. No longer burdened by fear or doubt, I had clarity I'd never known. I knew the language of the spirits and the messages they wished to portray; I saw my gifts as a source of strength, a gateway to knowledge, healing, and growth. And with each passing day, I forged a deeper bond with the unseen realms, weaving together the past, present, and future into a tapestry of transformation.

It was here that I knew I had found my place in the world, not as a victim of circumstance but as the victor of my destiny.

Now, I perceive time through a kaleidoscope of possibilities, each moment an integral color to the unique patterns that emerge. Time is not a rigid construct but a fluid medium, ever-present and infinitely malleable. It's the canvas upon which we paint our aspirations, a playground where the past, present, and future converge in a beautiful mosaic of potential. With this perspective, I now see every experience as a stepping stone and every setback as a chance for redemption. It is a constant reminder that in the grand theatre of life, we are both the playwrights and the actors, capable of shaping our destiny with every choice we make.

So, I embraced this new understanding of time, dancing with its ebbs and flows and relishing in its boundless opportunities. In this eternal loop of existence, I've learned that there is endless room for growth, transformation, and the pursuit of our highest selves. So much so that it's become the cornerstone of my life's work, guiding souls like mine to break free from the trappings of their past, transform their present, and help them craft a future that resonates with their deepest desires. Together, we can navigate this timeless journey, unlocking the boundless potential within each moment and forging a path toward true happiness when we reconnect to the here and now, in life's great life force, in the magic of the present moment.

So, here I stand. In wholeness, I am no longer afraid of being lost through time, no longer fearing my connection to the spirit world, no longer feeling broken, but rather seeing myself as a beautiful mosaic where my light can shine through even the smallest of cracks, knowing that the kaleidoscope of colors that reflects through each beam of light is mine to paint my life however I wish.

So, to anyone struggling to find where they belong, who may feel lost in their despair or disconnected from their life or the magic of their unique soul, I say this: you are not alone and have never been alone. You are stronger than you know, braver than you believe. And though the road to healing may be long, and the path may be winding, know that there is, and always has been, an ancient wisdom in your soul, a sense of wonder and power that courses through your veins. When all hope is gone, there is still light finding its way through the smallest of cracks, and whether you feel as though maybe your soul belonged in 1422, 1873, or 2056, the truth is that it does belong.

About Elle Embers

Elle Embers is a leading Soul Therapist, Quantum Energy Healer, Cosmic Channel, and captivating Host of the Cosmic Curiosities Podcast. With an unwavering commitment to guiding souls back to their innate magic and authenticity, Elle stands at the forefront of a profound paradigm shift in the realms of spiritual healing and personal transformation.

Through her intuitive gifts and mastery of energy work, Elle helps to clear blockages on a physical, mental, emotional, and energetic level. Her work allows her clients to realign with their highest state of balance and harmony, inviting them to embark on a journey of profound self-discovery and empowerment.

Through her groundbreaking work in timeline exploration, Elle's sessions offer a gateway to a reality where infinite possibility awaits. Her clients are invited to transcend the limitations of linear time, unlock the secrets of their souls, and unleash their inner magic. This process allows them to reprogram their limiting beliefs and manifest the life of their dreams, a journey that is both intriguing and empowering.

Elle's journey began in childhood, marked by profound inner exploration and transformative experiences. These pivotal moments led to a life-altering transformation, propelling her to a reality beyond her wildest dreams. She now resides in Queensland, Australia, embracing a life of fulfillment and purpose.

You can connect with Elle at Website: www.elleembers.com or Instagram: @elle.embers or Podcast: Cosmic Curiosities (Spotify & Apple Podcasts)

The Phone Call

By Ellie Blake

The Phone Call

"Hi, Ellie. It's Dr. Smith calling with your blood work results. Is now a good time?"

"Uh, yeah. Sure."

"Okay, great. I wanted to ask, were you fasting before going to the lab?"

"No, was I supposed to?"

"No, we didn't tell you to; I just wanted to check. Your results show that your prolactin levels are very high, which can indicate a tumor on your pituitary gland. I'd like to recheck your levels in two weeks. Please do fast this time."

I'm not sure if I even responded to her. It's possible I was able to muster up a meek "Okay" before hanging up.

Two weeks later, my prolactin levels had tripled, and the subsequent MRI of my brain revealed a tiny lesion right where she said it would be.

***

The Day Before the Phone Call

In the middle of the afternoon, I woke up in a hungover fog, having accomplished nothing the day before other than binge-watching Netflix and getting high all day in bed. Oh, and of course, drinking copious amounts of Miller Lite. I could point the finger at COVID-19 or keep it real and admit these were my usual antics for nearly a decade.

A Decade Before the Phone Call

From the outside looking in, you'd see a carefree party girl surrounded by friends, not knowing that often, the people who are never alone are the loneliest. I hid it well, or so I thought, but occasionally, I'd come across someone who saw through the facade.

"You seem to be running from something," or "I can tell you're hurting," someone I hardly knew would say to me. And I'd laugh it off as I took another shot or did another line.

I didn't care about anything or anyone, including myself. My top priority was out-partying everyone and making enough money to continue supporting this lifestyle and the habits that came along with it. Naturally, it made the most sense for me to be a bartender and, thus, immerse myself in the party scene 100% of the time.

I would wake up around 4 pm, get high, take a shot or two, go to work, continue partying, party after work until sunrise, pass out, and repeat for seven years.

Those years passed by in the blink of an eye. Occasionally, I'd wake up and wonder what happened to that determined little girl who wanted to go to an Ivy League college, own her own business, be an author, be a Mom, and travel the world. Another joint or beer, and I'd forget about her again, shoving her back into the abyss of my clouded mind.

A lot of people around me started dying. *An overdose? How embarrassing. Was it laced with fentanyl? That'll never happen to me.* I foolishly thought as I continued to do the same things with the same group of people as the ones whose lives were cut short.

"I wanna be your friend, but we can't be anything more than that. You party too much," my now husband had once told me. And for some reason, I cared.

Slowly, I cleaned up my act. I quit working at a bar and cut off people without explanation. I stopped doing hard drugs and not because I wanted him to like me, okay partially, but mostly because I knew he was right. All of the people who actually loved and cared about me were in the dark, and the ones who knew what I was up to, were just as fucked up as I was. He had seen the darkest parts of me and what I was up to daily and thought I could do better. Not only that, but he cared enough to tell me so.

To say I did a complete 180 at this point would be a lie. I still drank, although shots of Jameson were no longer a part of my morning routine. I still smoked weed, which I wholeheartedly believe is an herbal medicine, but admittedly, I was not using it for medicinal purposes at this point in my life. You can take away the scene, the people, the party, and all of it, but what still remains is a lost and broken version of you. And although my husband cared deeply, this part was for me to figure out. I was the only one who could.

And so I didn't for a few more years because sometimes it's easier to pretend there is no issue rather than digging deeper and facing it head-on. It can often lead to memories and feelings you are not interested in reliving. Sometimes, if you're lucky, you are forced to face your demons, though - like when your doctor calls you and tells you that you have a brain tumor.

The Day After The Phone Call

When Alexander Graham Bell invented the telephone, I don't think he anticipated the amount of singular phone calls that would irreparably change a person's life. This was the first moment in my adult life where there would forever be a distinct before and after.

My initial reaction was to burst into tears, followed by running downstairs and telling my husband that my doctor thinks I have a brain tumor.

"What?" he said in disbelief as he pulled me in for a hug. I remember him reassuring me that everything would be okay and that we should remain calm until we had more answers. "Let's not worry until we have something to worry about."

It was a total of five weeks from the phone call, the second round of lab work, and the MRI, which is an incredibly long time when you're convinced that you're going to die. Spoiler alert: I am alive and well. I was given medication that I took for a year to shrink the tumor, and I continued to have my prolactin levels checked regularly. Modern medicine is truly wonderful, but the magic that happened in those five weeks was the real miracle.

"So, I have a bitch ass brain tumor," I wrote in my journal. Journaling became a daily habit after the phone call. The little girl buried inside of me with dreams and goals always journaled, but it quickly fell to the wayside when drugs, alcohol, and boys were introduced into my life.

It was difficult to process all the thoughts and emotions running through my mind, but I desperately needed to express them instead of avoiding them. It was messy, full of spelling errors, run-on sentences, jumping from one thought to another, and at times, not making a whole lot of sense at all, but I just let it flow. Other times, I let it come to a complete stop when I was empty, and nothing more could be said. I was vulnerable, allowing myself to write down my truest thoughts and deepest fears without judgment.

I nurtured the little girl inside of me, and by doing that, all the scary thoughts and fears turned into dreams, goals, and desires. I accepted that I might soon find out I was dying, and instead of not caring at all, I decided to make the best of it. "If you only have a short time left, who do you want to be? What do you want to do? What will people say at your funeral? What do you want to leave the world with?" I wrote.

I meditated daily on it. I went on long walks outside and contemplated it. I physically tried new things, experimenting and allowing myself to suck at them and figure out what I liked and what wasn't for me. I drank hot lemon water and herbal teas. I started doing yoga. I practiced breathwork. I read novels for nothing other than pure enjoyment. I studied ancient concepts like Ayurveda, Dharma, and IKIGAI, as well as modern ones like Human Design and the Myers-Briggs Type Indicator. Learning as much about myself as possible taught me to love myself again. I accepted my quirks, embraced my strengths, and worked relentlessly on my weaknesses.

Simultaneously, I developed a deeply spiritual relationship with the universe. I could no longer see life through the same lens. I went from asking, "Why is this happening to me?" to, "How is this happening for me?" While I had the unwavering support of my loved ones, at the end of the day, all I have and all I'll ever have is me. I really wanted to like who I am and feel wholly supported by myself.

Through my self-discovery and personal development journey, I was able to answer the questions I asked in my journal. "I want to spread love and laughter through my writing and creativity." It seems fairly simple, broad even, but it is deeply personal. I had discovered my true passion and purpose in life.

Shortly after the phone call, I launched my business, an online greeting card shop called As Told By Ellie. I didn't concern myself with what others thought or even the logistics of it all. I had just risen from the lowest point of my life, and there was nothing that could stop me or that I couldn't figure out.

When you give yourself the power back and the permission to be bold and unapologetically follow your dreams, magic happens. Genuine Harry Potter shit, my friend.

As my health improved, my business continued to soar. Any obstacle I faced, I easily overcame. You see, I was never focused on the outcome because, for a while there, I didn't know if I'd live to see it. Instead, I focused on doing things that made me feel good every single day.

If you can change the way you think, the perspective from which you view things, and the lens through which you see life, you can change the reality that you live in. If that fails, just grow a brain tumor, and I'm confident you'll figure it out. Just kidding, sort of.

About Ellie Blake

Ellie Blake is a trailblazer who unashamedly champions her unique philosophy through her entrepreneurial ventures. As the dynamic CEO and founder of *As Told By Ellie*, a greeting card and gift company, she caters to an audience that appreciates humor with a twist of audacity.

Ellie started *As Told By Ellie* after walking through a potentially life-threatening health scare and realizing life is too short not to follow your dreams, and her super niched products s resonate with those who embrace their quirks and reject societal norms. In addition to her role at As Told By Ellie, Ellie also hosts the podcast, "F*ck *The Status Quo*," where she challenges conventional ideas and encourages her listeners to live authentically.

Ellie's primary mission is to infuse the world with love and laughter, while also daring to push societal boundaries. Her work consistently inspires others to proudly showcase their true selves, without fear or apology. Through her innovative business and outspoken media presence, Ellie has created a platform that not only entertains but also emboldens individuals to question the norm and find joy in their genuine identities.

Living in Florida with her husband and fur babies, Ellie inspires and empowers her audience to live life to the fullest.

You can follow and connect with Ellie at Instagram: @astoldby.ellie

Becoming the Author of My Life

By Georgie Hansen

There are many times in my life when I feel like I've emerged.

Sometimes, it feels more like being spat out of a fire hose and splattered on the floor than an elegant walk into the light.

When I think of an emergence, I'm instantly reminded of the butterfly and her chrysalis. And the metamorphosis, although magical, isn't necessarily pretty or graceful for the creature experiencing it. Its body tissue literally breaks down, liquefies, and reforms from a cylindrical shape into an entirely new creature with wings.

The emergence I want to share in this book is one where I physically transformed, much like the caterpillar becoming the butterfly via metamorphosis in her chrysalis.

I distinctly remember the exact moment I decided I would make this change.

It was a splenic whisper (which is how I receive my intuition). This intuitive voice/download/nudge dropped in the idea of having weight loss surgery.

Even though, at that point, I had put on more than 40kgs throughout five pregnancies, and I had tried all the diets, exercises, programs, eating plans, healthy weight loss systems, calorie counting, every single thing available to me, it had NEVER occurred to me that I would ever have surgery. That was not an option I had ever considered, entertained, or frankly thought was available to me.

So when this idea dropped in, it was almost like a brand-new concept and took me completely by surprise.

I immediately rang one of my good friends, who is also deeply intuitive and told her. She said, "Yes, this is what you are going to do."

I was in a carpark, waiting for my children to finish school, and I immediately started researching online.

It was the strangest thing. There were MANY obstacles or what most people would call 'blocks' in the way of this sudden decision coming to fruition.

It was early 2020, and thanks to Covid, the world had just shut down. All elective surgeries were suddenly canceled. I had just canceled my health insurance a few weeks earlier (because I only got it for the birth of my rainbow baby, who was then about 14 months and firmly planted on earth). I had four young children. I was running a business with my husband, and our main contract was under threat. I was in the process of starting my own business. I had just started a year-long intense intuitive guide certification program, and I wasn't sure if I could have surgery and go through recovery while also studying (and when I ran the idea by my mentor, she told me, "What a load of BS, I can't believe you're considering this."

All of these reasons why I COULDN'T or SHOULDN'T do this.

But what happened next is what I now realize is the art of and key to manifestation.

1. because the intuitive knowing/idea landed with such intensity and;

2. because I knew when it landed that it was a certainty, and there was NO RESISTANCE. I.e., my belief in the thing energetically matched the thing.

Intuitive knowing + non-resistance (belief matched) = Manifestation into existence

Suddenly, and very quickly, mind you, all of the ducks lined up.

I rang the health insurer, who re-enacted my policy immediately without a waiting period.

I did my research and found the right surgeon, who happened to have the best reputation in the country and was local to me. Even though the elective surgeries were being canceled, I was the first on his list when the ban was lifted a couple of months later.

I was able to access funds from my super to pay the out-of-pocket expenses.

I had the support of my husband.

I decided to stay in the intuitive guidance program. I continued my training while working in our business, still taking steps on my own business and looking after four kids with minimal disruption.

The surgery itself, and in terms of the intended goal, was 100% successful. I lost over 40kgs within the first six to nine months.

AND - it also took me on a completely different journey from what I was expecting.

Three months after the weight loss surgery, I started getting internal pain that escalated over a few days. By the time I landed in the emergency department, I was unable to walk from what felt like a giant lump on my perineum and pain, unlike I'd ever experienced. On the outside, it just looked and felt like a red and hot swelling, but I knew that was just the tip of the iceberg and something very wrong was happening internally. I was right.

A CT scan revealed an internal abscess about 10cm from the external red swelling on the skin surface. I was rushed into emergency surgery an hour later, at 10 pm, because I had already started to show signs of sepsis.

The abscess was cleared, and I was immediately out of pain. My surgeon told me there is a chance that it could return and about a 50% chance that if it does, it could cause something called a fistula.

Exactly a month post-surgery, my surgeon gave me a call to check in and see if I was healing ok. I said, "Yes, absolutely no pain or symptoms." He said, "Great! It looks like we've escaped the chances of a fistula occurring, and hopefully, that's it done and dusted, and I'll never hear from you again."

Oh, how wrong we both were.

The very next day, I felt a familiar pain return in my perineum. A swelling started again, which quickly, within hours, started to get hot, and I started to feel quite unwell. I rang the surgeon and told him my symptoms. He sighed and said I'm so sorry.

The next two years were spent in a grueling tormentation of a chronic health condition that was invisible to the world but all I could think about or focus on.

It brought me to my knees over and over again. I had the most dehumanizing experiences of seton insertions, vacuum extractors attached to my wound, at least ten more surgeries, multiple trips to the hospital for emergency infections and surgeries, and nurses on the ward who knew me by name because I was there so often. I wore a pad 24/7 for two years, was literally leaking gunk all day long, and had a giant inch-wide hole with a tunnel bored inside me that just kept getting bigger and bigger with each attempt to fix it.

About 18 months into this health journey, after one of my last surgeries, I had one of my dear friends come and visit me. We went down to the hospital cafe for a coffee, and she said, "What the hell are you doing? You're still doing all of these things,"

"You cannot go on doing what you do, helping everyone else, giving giving giving; your cup is beyond empty. It's like a bucket with a massive hole in it that's hemorrhaging gunk."

She was right, and I needed to hear it. My cup had a literal (physical and metaphysical) hole inside it. And I continued to plug it up and pour from it.

At that moment, I decided I needed to take a long, hard look at my life. I was about to launch a magazine a few months later; curiously, it was called "The Chrysalis Magazine," and at that moment, I made the hard choice to pull the launch.

I can't tell you that I magically stopped doing everything that kept me busy or became completely zen and healed because that would be a lie. I didn't suddenly know how to rest well, I didn't stop giving to everyone around me, and I certainly didn't suddenly learn the lesson of giving from an empty cup.

I also didn't immediately heal the fistula. There were many times when I was scared it would never heal. And sometimes, I wondered if I could continue to live if it didn't.

No one realized how much energy it took, how awful it was to live with an invisible health condition that impacted my whole life.

When I went anywhere with my children, I would have to plan ahead, make sure I knew where a bathroom was at all times, pack extra underwear and clothes (for me), be mindful of every activity and movement I made, on top of the recovery and aftermath, not to mention physical and emotional trauma, of invasive surgery after invasive surgery.

It took maybe another 1 or 2 surgeries (I've actually lost count) and at least another six months plus my first bout of COVID to finally and permanently heal that thing.

But it did **heal.**

And **I** did heal.

After I healed the fistula, I went on various other journeys of deep personal growth and expansion that were equally as uncomfortable as the physical metamorphosis that took place from the butterfly effect of the weight loss surgery, including a full nervous system shutdown, plus two more unrelated life-threatening medical emergencies requiring life-saving surgeries.

And that fistula taught me the most valuable lessons of my life, which, two and a half years later, I am only truly starting to fully embrace and embody.

1. *Rest begets success*: rest and healing are the opposite of weak. It also doesn't have to look typical. Rest comes in many forms.

2. *Strong boundaries create space*: having boundaries around time, energy, people, places, and spaces is the best way to create the space we need to align and heal.

3. *Focus and aligned action*: Coming into alignment,

mastering our mind, and taking intentional action towards our focus is the quickest way to success.

4. *Building a foundation of inner peace*: nothing else really matters without inner peace.

5. *Intuition over everything*: listening to your inner guidance and compass (which comes directly from Source/God/Universe) over anyone, anything, or any other source of information, is the ultimate key to making decisions for your highest good.

Sometimes in life, what we desire to manifest - manifests into something we cannot fathom or conceive.

Sometimes, what we bring into fruition is not what we thought we wanted but exactly what we needed, and therefore, becomes something even better than we could have imagined.

I know I'm not perfect, and no longer try to be. But this metamorphosis has led me to build a foundation of a deep, core inner peace.

I have learned to let go of what doesn't matter and hone in on what does. To become the Author of my life and to help other women be theirs.

We can create our own beautiful life story. Sometimes, it means manifesting exactly what we desire, and sometimes, it's learning to see things through a different lens. That's the power of shifting our perspective; that's the Miracle. So that no matter our experiences or circumstances, we can always control how we see things. To help them share their message, methodology, and mission for the service and deep transformation of others.

I am showing women how to create their own story, find the magic and abundance that already exists within them, and exponentially amplify it by sharing it wisely and intentionally with the world.

That's how we become the Author of our life.

Through this journey and the ones that have followed, I learned to properly fix that hole in my cup and to listen to the intuitive whisper that tells how to serve, and only from the overflow on the saucer.

About Georgie Hansen

Georgie Hansen is the CEO of Mosaic Media, a trailblazing publishing company with a mission to lead female entrepreneurs to share their mission, movement, and message and create the impact they know they are here for.

With 20 years in the media, communications, marketing, PR, and publishing industry, Georgie is a writer, editor, designer, and marketer with a deep understanding of energetic principles and practices. She combines her training in intuitive intelligence with proven heart-centered strategies and frameworks.

She has created a unique framework that simplifies the publishing process to make maximum impact and influence for women leaders. Through this book movement method, they distill their message, create a timeless legacy, and use their book as their marketing channel to scale their business beyond becoming a bestseller.

Georgie is not just an internationally bestselling author and publisher but also a passionate advocate for angel mamas. Her advocacy work has earned her features on various podcasts, summits, events, and top-tier publications.   ,

Georgie's life's work and mission is to empower women to be the Authors of their lives, to choose and shift their perspectives, and to create their own realities. She is a living example of this, choosing to live a beautiful life regardless of her tragic experiences in sunny Queensland, Australia, with her twin flame husband and four earth-side children. Her daughter in heaven serves as a guiding light, reminding Georgie of the importance of her mission.

Connect with Georgie at Website: www.mosaic-media.co or Instagram: @georgies_mosaic

Learning to Trust and Follow My Heart's Simple Guidance

By Jemma Redman

My heart has always known exactly what I need and the answers are always simple. Yet, going through the experiences that led me to trust and follow my heart's simple guidance felt painful, unfair, and often tormentingly complicated. Losing my father to suicide as a child and my first-born son at birth as a young woman became pivotal and necessary experiences to anchor deep trust within my heart. Both experiences broke my heart to the place where fear taunted my will to survive. I recall vividly the moments following each loss that I felt myself landing in that darkest place of my broken heart.

The most recent happening as a young, extremely ambitious, 28-year woman preparing to be a first-time mother who would be, do and have it all. I'd been successful in my career and started a side business to gain more time and freedom. I had everything planned and felt so in control, paying no attention to that little feeling at the bottom of my gut that I had too much on my plate. That was until everything changed so life-shatteringly fast, and the moment happened.

Coming out of the lift was like stepping back into the living hell I'd just been released from. As the doors opened, I saw the silver frame and plastic crib filled with one of those pink, blue, white, and yellow striped blankets. My broken heart sunk deep into my chest, and numbness flooded my entire body. I couldn't bear to look inside the crib, so I glanced up at the woman pushing it, her gaze fixated inside. Her face looked exhausted, yet her eyes beamed with life in a way that I desired deeply. Instantly, I felt suffocated by darkness closing in on me until disgust shielded me from defeat.

We walked out of the lift and into the foyer crowded with cribs, new mothers, and their doting families. My thoughts took nasty stabs at every mother I passed as my family ushered me toward the exit. "How dare these women flaunt their perfect newborn babies in the foyer of a specialist hospital where mothers lose their babies every day!" I snarled to myself. "What is wrong with these women?" I thought, "Do they not have a brain or a heart?!"

Walking towards the car, my shield began to crack, and darkness defeated me with its cold, double-edged sword going straight through me. I collapsed into painful pools of tears as flashbacks from the day before began to flood my mind. My son's tiny, perfect hand held tightly onto my finger as life left his body. Feeling my heart completely open and expand to hold his safely inside mine, then become wrapped in darkness. Memories so painfully beautiful, protected by the darkest fear, and created with the purest love left me stuck between avoidance and longing.

Losing the most precious thing my heart had ever loved and knowing there was nothing I could do to bring him back had become my reality. I had no plan for survival in the darkness, and my will to survive was at knifepoint. My armor had been stripped, and being seen as bare to the bone left me with no hope. I'd lost all sense of purpose, and everything I'd previously thought was important had fallen off with the armor. Now, my reality was sitting at the bottom of a deep, dark hole, bare-boned with no way out, wishing that the walls would collapse and bury me. I knew at that very moment I would never be the same again.

But I was comforted by a strange familiarity, as if I'd fallen down the hole long ago but had just forgotten I was there. I felt the same sense of helplessness and aloneness, sitting at the bottom of that hole after losing my dad when I was nine years old. The same life-shattering heartbreak that destroys all hope of happiness. Dad had abandoned Mum and me when I was born, but the hope of finding him one day gave me purpose and ignited my ambition. I used to fantasize about tracking him down, and once he saw how pretty, smart, kind, and caring I was, he'd never want to let me go again. I didn't care that he'd left us, only about finding him and being together.

One day, when I told my mum I was planning to find Dad, she got very upset. I remember feeling angry at her that what I longed for was upsetting her, so I declared to myself that I'd find him without her; that was until she told me. My heart stopped beating for a moment as I sat in disbelief. Mum reaffirmed to me that my Dad had died a short time ago and his heart had 'gone on him.' I felt my heart begin to slowly shatter as I recalled a night when Mum received a distressing phone call and locked herself in her room. I heard her cry, but she refused to tell me what was wrong. As I realized Dad had died that night, my dreams were crushed in an instant. I felt so betrayed, angry, and devastated that he would never get to love me the way I'd been yearning for as long as I could remember.

Later that night, the moment happened, and I landed in the darkest part of my broken heart, sitting at the bottom of that deep dark hole, bare-boned, wishing the walls would collapse and bury me. I was in the bath, balling my eyes out, when my young brother, who would have been two at the time, came in to comfort me. Envy became my first piece of armor as I screamed at him to leave me alone; his father was still alive, and that did not feel fair. My body felt so shielded by envy that I couldn't see the care inside his young and pure heart.

My memories become vague and distant from that moment on, but it makes sense now that I progressively found my way onto the path of addiction. Slowly, I began building a suit of painkilling armor to keep me from ever feeling the darkest part of my heart inside the bottom of that hole. Beginning with food, then money, possessions, alcohol, and eventually drugs. Behind my armor, I couldn't see the pain I was causing others or my body. But as I began to mature, causing others pain often resulted in rejection and heartbreak, taking me briefly to the place inside my heart I feared most.

So, I started taking off the parts of my armor that hurt others and strengthened the rest with perfectionism and achievement. Believing my suit of armor had become impenetrable through how my life looked and what I had achieved gave me hope as I climbed towards the light, forgetting about the darkness inside that hole. Yet the more I believed in the power of my suit, the heavier it felt, and the deeper the hole got. Maintaining my life felt burdensome, the effort increasing with each step towards the light, only to have the top get further away. This is where I found myself as a 28-year-old woman preparing to become a mother who would be, do, and have it all, convinced each next step would be the last out of the hole.

Having a lifetime of armor stripped away and falling to the bottom of that hole again felt like everything I'd been through and sacrificed in my life until now was for nothing. I knew how to do nothing else than to build my suit of amour strong again or succumb to the darkness and die. Whilst dying often felt like an easier option, I knew first-hand how it felt to lose someone to suicide, and I couldn't bear to send others to the darkest part of their hearts, so I tried to build my armor strong again. I fought hard to get back to a 'normal' life, but the more I ignored the pain inside my heart, the more I needed those old pieces of armor that hurt others again. I quickly reverted to drinking and drugs to numb that feeling inside my gut that something wasn't right and keep focused on climbing. I wasn't yet ready to accept that the life I'd created, wearing my armor suit, would keep me stuck inside that hole forever. My heart knew that, but I wasn't yet able to listen.

After our son's passing, my husband and I retreated to an old caravan for two weeks on my grandparent's property so we had space to grieve. It was old and dingey but had a simple charm. I felt safe there, unbothered by its imperfection, rejuvenated by nature, supported by nearby family, and temporarily freed from the heaviness of my armor suit. During our stay, I fantasized about living there, just like I did as a child about finding Dad. This desire came from deep within my heart, making no sense but easy and magical, like a sacred knowing that the caravan was where my heart wanted me to be. I had heard my heart's simple guidance toward my true desires for the first time since childhood but felt unsafe trusting it without a realistic plan beyond living in that caravan. My armor suit, although extremely heavy, had kept me safe for so long, and I feared what others would think of me if I let go of it to see me bare-boned.

I held on tight to my armor suit for another nine months before the hole started to collapse. I was suffering from PTSD and couldn't go back to work. We were fighting a losing battle to get out of our franchise side business, and I was getting high every day just to survive. The collapse was worsening by the day, and I'd become so weighed down by my armor that the only way to survive was to take it off. So we sold the business at a huge loss, sold our house to get out of debt, I left my career in the city, and we moved down the coast into the old caravan. Although fearing it looked like I was waving my white flags, as I took my armor off, I made my way out of that collapsing hole and felt the light surrounding me.

Now, I can also vividly recall the moment I felt the light I hold within my heart; it was the day we arrived at the old caravan to start our new life. Walking down the steep grassy bank, fear tormented me with the thought of how many times I might slip down this new daily route. I felt the familiar pattern of stress tense across my forehead, and my body began to brace for impact. I noticed an obsessive urge to plan how to fix the slope as if I were reaching for armor to protect me. I knew if I followed the urge, I'd get lost in an endless crusade of unrest, perfecting the imperfect. So, instead, I looked up and into the bush ahead filled with tall, sturdy gum trees and thick Australian bush stretching to the mountains. With no neighbors in sight, yet knowing family and other familiar faces were not far away, I breathed the serenity and safety into my heart, and as I breathed out, I felt presence and trust spread from my heart to my entire body.

It's taken time to discover how to connect with the light I hold within my heart and receive its simple guidance. Still, the stronger I grow the connection between my mind and heart, the more I magically create my true desires with ease and grace. Experiences of adversity now allow me to connect deeper with my heart while I navigate the darkness with grace, knowing the light will return even brighter, trusting in all challenges to raise my energetic capacity to hold my desires. My journey has taught me a deep awareness of my mind's attachment to gathering armor, and when I allow it, my reality becomes a heavy struggle. But I have become a compassionate observer and know the path back to my heart where I receive simple direction. Sometimes, it doesn't make immediate sense, but it always feels easy and eventually makes complete sense when my desires magically unfold.

Both memories of my darkest heartbreak, losing my son and my dad, have evolved from nightmares I avoided to memories that fill my heart with gratitude and purpose. Landing in the darkest part of my heart gave me an opportunity to experience the contrast and trust my heart to lead me. As a woman and mother, I've witnessed in awe the impact being attuned to my heart has on those around me, and so it has become my mission to teach mothers how to trust their heart's simple guidance to transcend adversity, embody their true essence and lead them to their true desires with ease and grace. As mothers, we are the heart of our family and community; through our heart attunement, we provide safety for others to disarm and discover trust in their hearts, too.

About Jemma Redman

Jemma, creator and teacher of the Heart Attunement Code, is a compassionate and inspired heart-led leader who believes in the magical possibilities for every mother, family, and community through the power of heart attunement.

Deeply embodied in her evolution, Jemma has nearly two decades of experience guiding and developing structures to facilitate personal and professional behavioral change.

Her experiences of deep loss, trauma and heartbreak led her to create a modality that forges a deep trust of the heart's intelligence, for mothers who yearn to meet their true desires and become heart-led leaders of their lives, families, and communities with ease and grace. Her wisdom and compassion teach and hold space for mothers to unravel from their complex minds, discover ease and safety, and develop trust in following their hearts' simple desires.

Jemma lives on the South Coast of NSW with her husband and two earthside children, who are supported by her community and nurtured by nature. She adores kookaburras; you will surely hear their call in her videos. Her angels, son Harrison, and father Brett, inspire and guide her towards connection and purpose in their legacy.

You can connect with Jemma at Website: jemmaredman.com or Instagram: @jemma.redman or Facebook: jemmamaeredman

Resilient Emergence

By Nyree Johnson

I entered the world in 1985 and called Sarina, Queensland, home. The home my Mum and Dad lived in was filled with love for me. A mere 15 months later, my sister, Carly, joined me. With Railway work responsible for our hometown choice, a few years later, my sister and I returned to our second hometown of Rockhampton in Central Queensland with our Mum after my parents separated. Surrounded by family and abundant love, I never noticed what we lacked financially.

Spending my early childhood and primary years moving from home to home in government housing meant I could explore different suburbs of Rockhampton. Moving day was always exciting because I was ready for the next adventure and new environment. Some might consider the disruption unstable, but for me, it was exhilarating. In my adult years, I realized moving as frequently as we did wasn't a familiar experience for most people I was surrounded by. Nevertheless, those life events began the building blocks of resilience and adaptability because it didn't matter what environment I was in; the only option was to make it work.

At seven years old, I welcomed a baby brother. With a different Dad to me and a shade of skin far darker thanks to his Aboriginal descent, Dominic was the apple of my eye, and I doted on him. Often scalded by Mum for waking him up to play, the disappointment came because he was always mid-nap when I felt compelled to make noise, dress him up, and play.

At the same age of seven, the first hurdle of my life arose when an older male neighbor inappropriately conducted himself, stealing my innocence of youth. Thanks to my Mum's wise words of stranger danger' and her repeated mantra of, "If someone tells you not to tell your Mum or Dad, you absolutely tell your Mum or Dad," a stop was put to the antics immediately, and the Police were notified. While Mum and Dad shielded me from the proceedings aside from a video-recorded testimony I delivered, the ordeal was over, but what followed changed my life forever for the better.

At seven years old and with no sporting ability, my Dad promptly enrolled me in the martial arts sport of Tae Kwon Do, and for the next 14 years, I practiced the art on and off. I am strong, confident, self-assured, and brave because of the discipline and values instilled in me by this sport. While my running style as a primary school student provided great entertainment to my family, it was obvious that athletics and ball games at school weren't my thing. But if you asked me to throw a shot put or fight, I was your girl.

Venturing into high school with a small group of friends from my small primary school, I experienced an adjustment period when entering a much larger school environment. Evidence of the adaptability I'd developed was obvious as I began to find my feet in this new environment, testing the boundaries and barely skating through academically. I later realized that the high school environment wasn't the right fit for me. With further education, I now understand that the system is tailored to one type of learner, which was different from me.

As a confident person and an extremely protective sibling, I found strife at school when aiding my sister against the bullies who taunted her. At the time, I didn't realize my strength, and even though I was taught to defend myself and never attack, a physical attack on my sister meant an inner monster was unleashed, which unfortunately resulted in my suspension from school at 15 years old.

With Dad cheering my actions and Mum begging for forgiveness from the Principal, it was due to her apologies and assurances that I could continue with the end of Junior High School events, which was lucky because that was where my schooling ended. While an attempt at Year 11 was made at a different school, my heart and head weren't in the game, and in hindsight, it was because the environment was not suited to my learning style.

At 15, I met my best friend and now husband, Nathan. From the start, I couldn't see my life without him, and since we met, we've been building a life together. As with every journey, it's been filled with happiness and heartache, sometimes simultaneously. My rock, though, is our relationship's consistency and mutual respect. If one of us is operating at 10%, the other is at 90%, and we do our best to balance each other out.

Nathan and I had a lot of fun with friends and in cars when we were younger. Over six months, though, this turned south. Many of us were reckless, and we lost some of our friends in car accidents, which prompted us to move away from Rockhampton and change our scenery while developing our maturity. We were the lucky ones, and to this day, we think of our friends who are no longer with us.

As horrific as some of our life stories are, realizing they had to be that way to develop us into who we are today proves to be a bittersweet sentiment.

At 16 and with Nathan by my side, we moved 700 kilometers west of Rockhampton to the small town of Longreach, with the drawcard being my Dad. As the local Baker, my Dad was well-established in the town and welcomed us to country living. In Longreach, I began my corporate career. I obtained my first post-junior High School qualification – a Certificate III in Business Administration, completed on the job while working for the local council. I'd found my learning style to be learning by doing and through relevant content to the real world.

At 18, it was time to transition to the next adventure. As we weren't quite ready to go home to Rockhampton, we set our eyes towards Brisbane, Queensland, where my Mum and her partner lived. Welcoming us into her home until we found our feet, we spent the next six years crafting our lives as adults, a married couple, and parents.

Our state's capital city provided many career and development opportunities for Nathan and me. It provided me with a well-rounded and transferable skillset that, again, traced back to the agility embedded in childhood. Backed by confidence and resilience, which were helpful in the ever-evolving corporate business world, I found my feet. Taking great pride in my presentability, productivity, and professionalism, I enjoyed a rewarding career in Brisbane until the Global Financial Crisis when my role was made redundant.

Being made redundant can impact confidence. It is important to practice self-compassion and avoid negative self-talk when this occurs. Knowing your worth and value is important, and understanding that your job does not define you is essential. Setbacks are part of everyone's career journey. When we reach retirement age and look back, it'll be with the same gratitude we do now for the journey we've traveled so far, whatever stage that is at. Each event contributes to how we become the people we are, and we need the challenges to rise, learn, and grow.

The timing of this redundancy was quite perfect as I was pregnant with my second child and would shortly discover a severe and hereditary medical condition that would impact the rest of my life. Everything happens for a reason, they say. Initially, not being able to walk was considered to be a pregnancy-related issue, but shortly after delivering my second child via an emergency cesarean, it was discovered that the condition remained even though my son had exited. A diagnosis of Spondylosis was presented alongside Scoliosis and Arthritis. What followed was years of movement restrictions, flare-ups, hospitalizations, and fumbling through medication, exercise, education, and recovery, all while building a career and raising a family.

My family and I make allowances for the physical restrictions and the pain management routine I maintain. What I don't do, though, is use my condition to stop me from living the life I want to, and instead, I use it to fuel my ambition of living the best life possible. The discipline derived from Tae Kwon Do can be attributed to my mindset of persistence and achievement. Rather than rely solely on a perfect set of circumstances to follow my destined path, I actively seek opportunities and look for the next chapter, trusting my intuition to take me where I need to be.

During the years following the Global Financial Crisis and while raising two young children, the pull home became strong, and we decided to return to Rockhampton in Central Queensland. With an array of skills and experiences to offer, my career didn't skip a beat, with copious opportunities and the addition of our third child. Having never had a role I disliked, I've always crafted a job to suit myself and led from where I was at the time.

'Leading from where you are' is one of my favorite mantras. Put simply, in any role within any organization, you can grab hold of your job description, develop it, and lead. Leading from where you are can take many forms. It can include leading your personal development, leading from within your team, setting great examples, and helping others along their personal development and professional journey.

Leading from where you are is about having the confidence, skills, self-awareness, and understanding to support your team and organization in achieving their goals. It's about knowing yourself, understanding your strengths and individual talents, and leading from whatever position you are in.

The perfect role, job, organization, or opportunity may never come along, and you simply can't sit and wait for 'your turn'; take it now, grab it yourself, and make it happen because your profile and reputation will thank you for it.

Being a Leader in your career is not about having the job title; it's about how you live your job. You don't need to manage people to be a Leader. You need to identify how you interact with the world around you, add value, work with your team, drive positive outcomes, and constantly ask yourself what else you can contribute to set a great example.

Choosing how you navigate your career and opportunities will enable you to progress toward personal goals while delivering on business goals without relying on anyone else.

Of course, workplaces are never all roses, and at times, we need to work with undesirable people, people who actively do the wrong thing, and people who abuse their positions.

One of the challenges I've faced in my career is where subtle yet harmful behaviors such as unwanted advances and manipulative comments were prevalent. This workplace, designed for high-performance productivity and teamwork, became a setting for personal and emotional trials hidden beneath a façade of routine operations. My experience, though not unique, highlights the complex dynamics of workplace abuse and the importance of recognizing and addressing these issues. It can be hard to escape, though, when your livelihood and career are in the hands of the perpetrator.

For those who find themselves in this situation, if you take nothing else out of this contribution to Emergence, please follow these guidelines. Of course, it's not an exhaustive list, but it's a start. Document everything, save emails, write about interactions and how they made you feel, and take screenshots where appropriate. If suitable, build a support network within your organization and use resources like Human Resources or other formal support networks. If you're in a Union, engage them as well. Read your workplace agreement, know your rights at work from a state and federal government level, understand the code of conduct all employees are expected to adhere to and follow the correct reporting chain to deal with such circumstances, bypassing where required if the supervisory chain of command involves the perpetrator.

Most of all, back yourself, and when you present your evidence, remain unemotive and solutions-focused. This will ensure the most successful outcome. Remember that you may not be able to control what is happening to or around you, but you can control your response.

When we feel called to seek help to move past a challenging moment or to heal from events, it's essential to realize that finding the proper help is critical. There is a lot of help available from professionals, support groups, and peers, but if what you've seen isn't working, remember that it's not you; it's them.

Often, people search for help and venture down the path of a counselor their doctor has recommended or a psychologist their employee assistance program has offered; however, just because a person has the qualifications to help doesn't mean they can help you. Please don't fall into the trap of thinking you're unworthy of help. It's only a matter of timing before you find the right fit, so don't give up.

When I was ready to ask for help in transitioning past a hurtful time in my life, four people came first before I found the perfect fit. Once you find the right fit, you'll instantly know you're in the right place, and the healing can begin.

Think of the journey as stripping bare all of the parts of you that cause shame, humiliation, and embarrassment, addressing and making peace with every trigger, even if it takes months. Then, your new scaffolding and frame can begin. The foundation of a solid structure lies in the sections you can't see, whether it's a building or a person. It's the unglamorous part of you where all the work has been done, which enables you to stand tall.

The most significant opportunity to improve ourselves and our lives exists in our minds. With the right help, the first priority to address healing and recovery exists with mindset and intention. These two allow us to have some control over how we navigate the world and our response to what happens around us and to us. Our mindset and intention prepare us for what life has in store each day. Once we create the habits of success and daily practices required, the clouds float away, the weight lifts and the world opens up with unimaginable opportunities because we've removed the limiting beliefs our life experiences to date have restricted us to.

For me, first came help, then healing, then control over mindset and intention, and an immense amount of gratitude for my life and journey, the good, bad, and ugly. From there, I began an enriching journey of self-education. Thanks to experience, age, and self-awareness of how I best learn, understanding what worked for me, and how I could best benefit from the world's experiences, I dove into education.

I actively sought development days, in-person and online courses, formal qualifications, and books unrelated to my career objectives. However, admittedly, they did compliment me. Each education opportunity was just for me. I want to develop myself, which pays dividends to my career, small business, and community. My intention has only been, and will only ever be, for me. I don't learn for others or because someone tells me to. I don't do what I do for any reason other than to ensure that tomorrow, I am a better person with more knowledge than who I am today.

While I also had the opportunity to develop professionally through workplace-based courses and training, this simply complimented the journey I was already on. One interesting aspect of a learner experience I observed in the workplace was how much content consumption occurred when a person had been voluntold to attend or nominated by their supervisor. It wastes everybody's time when you're not actively engaged in the content delivered because you are not interested in being there—yours, the trainers, and your employers.

Instead, when a cringeworthy workplace opportunity does arise, you can change your mindset and approach to extract anything valuable from the content. If you genuinely have to attend a course you're not interested in, spend some time before it falls to set an intention for yourself to ensure you save time. Even if you walk away with one different technique or lesson, it is worth it.

Curiously, when I began my deep dive into education, I also started observing the world far closer than ever, realizing that everyone in life is a teacher. They're either teaching me what to do or what not to do, whether they realize it or not. As with all well-meaning advice, you take what you need from the lesson and discard the rest.

Help, healing, mindset, gratitude, and education are a bittersweet combination of essential elements that trigger an Emergence.

Profound self-awareness and a deliberate journey bring the confidence to genuinely follow your path and the courage to say yes to opportunities as they arise. It's a constant state of preparedness so that when you're presented with a fork in the road, you have the confidence to take the challenging path, knowing that it's in those moments of discomfort and challenge where the magic lies and true personal growth exists.

An unexpected political opportunity presented itself to me, and thanks to the journey I'd been on, after a brief consultation with two trusted people, I said yes to the encouragement I received. While the outcome didn't appear to be a success in the traditional sense, the lessons learned, opportunities gained, friendships and family relationships changed forever positively, and the connections that were established and continue to grow meant that it was a success to me.

The campaign cost $20,000, and the professional and personal development resulting from the experience fast-tracked what should have taken years to achieve and condensed it into an intensive masterclass spanning two and a half months.

The two people I consulted regarding decision-making form part of my inner circle. It's not a large circle; only two people are in it. Knowing who to trust and confide in is crucial to maintaining a solid foundation to launch at opportunities. The support network knows you better than you know yourself at times. Above all else, they're the people you listen to because you know they have your best interests at heart. They're the type of person you can unpack tricky situations with, and they'll tell you what you need to hear, not what you want to hear.

Choosing an inner circle takes years of relationship-building and testing. Sometimes, our circle will float in and out of our lives, and that's okay, too, because, like us, they're enjoying their life journey too. Different priorities or life events will result in their availability shifting over time. It's essential to see this for what it is and not take it personally when someone you once were close to isn't as close anymore.

With growing children, an array of community initiatives and participation, a small business to manage, and a career to nurture, it's more important than ever to recognize that while I pride myself on working hard, I play harder.

I live passionately and pursue the things I enjoy. From volunteering to writing, Rum nights with friends, drag racing, car festivals, family, and camping, I immerse myself in opportunities to play and have fun, living by the mantra, ' Work hard, play harder.'

While there might be a lot going on from the outset, and I won't discount that there is, I must convey that these things aren't happening simultaneously. They're intentionally imbalanced because I refuse to entertain the notion of work-life balance. It simply does not exist when living an extensive and full life.

An *Intentional Imbalance* is a way of merging your roles and responsibilities. It is a philosophy that ensures you can do what you love and do what you need to so you can be involved in what you want to be all at once. It requires an element of organization and emotional intelligence, with some resilience and strength mixed into the equation. Of course, this only comes naturally to some of us and requires focus, development, and practice.

An Intentional Imbalance means you can say yes! to being and doing you while accommodating your commitments and responsibilities and leveraging your skillset.

I'm not a Superwoman and will never claim that title. It's not about being an overachiever or about overdoing it. It's about doing what you love and aligning yourself with what makes you happy and fulfilled. What I involve myself in aligns with my values and brings joy. I know what I want in life and how to achieve it. Having worked hard on clarity and self-awareness over the years, even when I feel lost or muddled, I know what it takes to pull myself out and keep moving forward. Strength, determination, discipline, and resilience are traits I've developed due to life experiences and deliberate development.

It's also essential to recognize that peak performance and intentional imbalance come with crucial rest requirements. While I am not a peak-performing elite athlete, I do put my mind to the test. Because of this, rest is essential to operating consistently at the frequency with which I like to work, live, and play.

- 10 minutes per day

- One hour per week

- One day per month

- One long weekend per quarter

- One holiday per year

It's that simple.

You can read more about this formula in one of my favorite books, The Third Space by Dr Adam Fraser. An entire chapter is dedicated to rest—Chapter 8 if you're interested. I followed his formula for rest and did it long before reading it in his book because I'd worked it out. I'd paid attention and knew what I needed to do to consistently perform.

As with any efficient business, implementing changes in your life to positively make a difference in how you show up in the world and emerge means setting up systems and good habits after the inner work and healing have been done. It can begin in parallel, but the maximum value is evident when the pre-work is complete. In addition, being realistic about every situation you're faced with will help you make the right call regardless of whether it's popular. By building resilience and self-confidence, you have the power to change the world, even if it's just for one person.

Sharing with others and empowering people to be the best versions of themselves brings great joy to my life. While I don't work in the coaching field, this desire is driven by a keenness to connect, collaborate, and celebrate with others. After all, we humans are not meant to experience this world on our own.

I share a monthly email with writing pieces, thoughts, experiences, and perspectives on my learning. If you're interested in connecting with me to receive this monthly email, please visit www.nyreejohnson.com.au, where you can sign up and find all of my social links.

About Nyree Johnson

Nyree Johnson is a prolific writer with an impressive array of publications and is a staunch advocate for her community.

In her professional life, Nyree excels by embracing challenges and changes, consistently delivering exceptional results. She combines a deep understanding of business dynamics with a proactive approach, enabling her to thrive in diverse environments. Beyond her career and small business, Nyree is deeply committed to community service. She serves as the District Commissioner for the Capricorn Scouts. She contributes her time and expertise as a committee member for other not-for-profit organizations.

Nyree is a prolific writer with an impressive array of publications, with a life philosophy that centers on living intentionally and with passion. She manages an "intentional imbalance" that allows her to excel across all aspects of her life. She skilfully integrates her roles, ensuring they align with her values and passions.

At her core, Nyree holds dear the values of compassion, respect, and a commitment to promoting diversity and equality. She inspires her community, tirelessly working to empower, build resilience, and support initiatives that create a safer, more inclusive community.

She resides in Central Queensland, Australia, with her husband, Nathan, and their three children. Nyree's career spans various sectors, blending corporate roles with entrepreneurial ventures, where she has developed a reputation for her adaptability and strategic acumen.

For those interested in exploring more about Nyree's journey or seeking to connect -

> Visit her website https://nyreejohnson.com.au/ which offers a gateway to a monthly newsletter and links to her socials. Nyree is always eager to engage with individuals who share her interests and aspirations.

Forged By Fire

By Paulina Smith

Various cultures traditionally associate black diamonds with transformation and spiritual growth. They were believed to catalyze personal evolution, aiding individuals in overcoming life's obstacles and becoming more resilient. The deep hue of black diamonds symbolizes the profound depths of the soul, showcasing inner strength and untapped potential.

My own journey of Undoing, Being, and Becoming has cracked me open again and again to slowly unfurl and reveal my very own black diamond heart, forged by the pressures, fires, and many composites in the ceremony of my life. Learning to keep my heart open through the valleys and peaks of my various life experiences, from profound joy to heartbreaking grief, has been slowly polishing the facets of my soul, bringing me home to mySelf. To awaken to the depths of my heart and embody the wisdom gained from my spiritual and personal transformations. Embracing the fact that I must embody surrender, trust, and faith in God and the unfolding of my life. In my journey of Becoming, I have been developing inner strengths, self-confidence, self-love, and empowerment to emerge with the strongest and most resilient heart. To simply become more Me.

The process of Undoing indicates I have had to walk the spiral of grief, letting go, accepting, and surrendering, in order to be completely emptied to create the spaciousness needed for the cultivation of what is yet to become. The stage of Being is where I face the reality of the event that has happened, take self-responsibility, where I have played either a conscious or an unconscious role in my current circumstances, and make peace with what I cannot control. I have to accept the feelings that can come along with the sense of loss of control.

This series of Undoing, Being, and Becoming represents the current of the life, death, and rebirth cycles inherent in nature and within our own journey as human beings.

My journey began at age four when I was diagnosed with leukemia and survived cancer. Doctors still talk about my case because I had defied the odds. Ever since, along with the grace of my parents, I was drawn to the mystical world and saw life with so much joy and wonder. I've had an uncanny ability to say, "Yes!" to experience life itself. What I hadn't wanted to accept as part of opening my arms wide open to life was the challenging, heart-breaking, painful experiences that are part of the package deal. By committing to toxic positivity and avoiding grief and anger, I shut down the connections to my emotions, to my intuitions, and to my magic. I put my energy towards other people, conforming even more to the conditioning role of a people pleaser. I was responsible, easy-going, and level-headed, and I often strived for perfection and to be liked and accepted. However, I didn't want to accept the shadows within myself that were keeping me in a state of soul dissociation. My ego and many other parts took hold and became in charge of my everyday life. The problem was I didn't even realize it because that was the cultural norm.

In 2019, when I had a spiritual awakening during a medicine ceremony, I was shown my second child, my daughter. I was shown the power within me and the relationship to God that I had been denying for most of my life. My relationship with God was abandoned when I attended a Catholic high school, and I graduated as a self-declared atheist. I would always say to myself, "I don't understand religion or God, but if this is what it is- I don't want any part of it!" Yet, I would say in the same breath, "However, I believe in the Universe and spirituality."

In my integration from the ceremony, I was shown how much I had denied myself, self-sabotaged, and had been an active yet very unconscious participant in the way I had been navigating my life. Holding onto people, places, and things that were not serving me led me to give up part of myself to be loved or accepted. I was shown how I had been a people pleaser to my own detriment, where I had been giving my own power away because I feared rejection and abandonment. I would tell myself that I was strong and could shoulder other people's burdens because I could. I didn't understand that I was taking on and in other people's energies and emotions, transmuting them within myself so that they would feel better. I was unaware that it would continue to make me feel worse, more anxious, and more disconnected from myself.

I thought it was my responsibility to take away other people's pain and relieve their suffering because I could. Because of the gift I was given for new life from surviving cancer, I thought it was my responsibility to save people from themselves. I didn't know that it was actually disempowering to others as much as it was having an impact on me. I also didn't know I was "allowed" to have a spine and have boundaries, let alone that it is my ethical responsibility to protect and uphold these healthy boundaries. I had allowed everyone else to shape my reality, even though I was under the pretense that I was the one calling the shots. Many of my decisions were shaped and formed by other people's emotional responses and desires out of my unconscious ego survival. I didn't want to feel uneasy in the presence of others' uneasiness. It wasn't always the case, but when I would be experiencing periods of low self-confidence, I would simultaneously receive criticism, judgments, or projections from others. I internalized all of what others said as truth, which would cause a spiral of self-doubt, shame, and guilt. Being so well conditioned in my role of perfection and people-pleasing, I would never question the clarity and integrity of the person making such declarations about me. I would immediately go over what I did wrong, how I was a bad person, and what to do to fix it.

There is a delicate balance between taking self-responsibility and maintaining curiosity about what others' statements are showing us about them. Projective identification was consuming my reality, thus perpetuating my disconnection from my soul essence and giving more leverage to my ego identity. It was very difficult to discern when I didn't have a connection to the strength of my inner core, know where my growth edges were, or be steadfast in knowing my energetic boundaries. I allowed my energy to leak out onto others and let others' energy pour into mine. I had severe acne and was very anxious– even in all of my foundational work as a psychotherapist. I didn't want to be seen, and I didn't trust in the flow of life, I was trying to control it. My acne was showing me the repressed anger that was deep under the surface that was literally seeping out of my pores. In fact, I would pride myself in how much I could take on, how selfless I could be, and how giving of my love and nurturance I could share. My perfectionism and fear of getting something wrong would paralyze me and even drive me to focus more on others than myself.

What did I need to do to nurture myself when I was feeling anxious and dissociated from being in the presence of others' pain? How could I tend to myself instead of overextending myself to appease or release others from their own life experiences? I was so busy caring and being present for other people that I didn't even realize "I" was missing.

What exactly was missing? The self-love of my own heart and soul. The authentic version of me that needed to do LESS and not more. To see myself and others as already whole. I could put down the roles and identities to allow my true nature to shine and inspire others by simply being myself versus what I thought I needed to do or be for someone else. To release others from my energetic control, no matter how well intentioned it was or appeared to be, to free myself and others to be the true conscious leaders within our own lives. To awaken to my inner Truth, "I am a spiritual being having a human experience, AND a human being having a spiritual experience."

The pregnancy of my daughter in 2020 catapulted me into everything I know now as the journey of the Divine Feminine. My role as a mother of two wild and strong souls urged that I learn to come back to listening to my intuition and heal the layers of generational trauma and societal conditionings. My intuition guided me to study under my mentor, Marin Bach-Antonson, and become a Priestess, a vow of being an emissary of Divine Mother's unconditional love. Discovering that unconditional love didn't mean putting myself, my needs, my desires, my intuition, on the back burner. It didn't mean self-sacrifice to the point of not recognizing myself. It didn't mean twisting myself into a pretzel to relieve others from their suffering. It did mean, however, that how I help people is more so in helping myself, giving myself permission and boundaries to say yes or no, or to re-evaluate consistently what truly continues to be in energetic and self-love alignment.

I became increasingly aware of how I was constantly abandoning and betraying myself and my own needs and how I would dim my light to make others feel more comfortable. I found myself experiencing the wild phenomenon of awakening to the layers of illusion I was living in. Awakening to my intuition, to my soul essence, to life as a ceremony, to the oneness of people and our earth, to God and Spirit.

The many cycles of Undoing, Being, and Becoming that I would continue to experience all contributed to the pressurization of my black diamond heart. Guiding me to deepen and lean more into listening to the guidance of God, my spirit guides, and my intuition. In 2021, I ushered my family to move to Hawaii after having a deeper internal pressure from Spirit to do so. I was becoming more sensitive and aware of my inner landscape, learning to listen to my soft, quiet inner voice and the wisdom my body was trying to share with me. I felt guided by God to march into the unknown. It made ZERO logical sense to move away from the stability of jobs, house, family, and childhood roots to step into the unknown and unchartered waters of the Big Island. Let alone try to explain this "soul calling" to my husband, family, and friends.

The energy of the Big Island, due to its rich history and volcanic activity, is intense and powerful, and it unearths the shadows we have long buried deep. The grief of unexpectedly losing my father, with whom I had a conflicted relationship with due to his alcoholism, shortly after moving to the island broke me down and cracked open in more ways I was prepared for. Losing three additional loved ones within the same year compounded the grief and continued to burn down what was no longer in alignment in my life and illuminate the path toward authenticity and soul embodiment.

I've learned that the internal conflicts I have within myself are played out in external relationships and life situations that I then have to reckon with when these conflicts are left in the shadows of the unconscious. I discovered that understanding my ethical responsibility of becoming self-aware, finding forgiveness for past mistakes, and learning to surrender my ego in order to allow God and Spirit's directions to come through all became the codes of my true sense of freedom. Through the lenses of various ancient and modern spiritual teachings, psychological theories, scientific findings of resonance and frequency, and quantum physics, I went on a soul-expanding journey to reclaim and rediscover all of who I am. Beyond ego constructs, generational traumas, and familial and societal conditioning is a beautiful path that is God and Spirit-led when I am open, attuned, and surrendered enough to allow it in.

Straightening out my spine, one vertebrae at a time, elongating my neck, and allowing my shoulders to relax down, I carry around with me the secret gift of being in love with my life. All of it. That is my wish and hope for humanity: to remember the truth of our divine essence and awaken to our unique, beautiful expression of love itself. To be fully aware of our divinity and love of self and others is true generational wealth and the best gift to bestow to our children.

My true journey has been learning to accept the cycles of life, integrate and embody the lessons for my soul growth, and keep my heart open while being shaped during the pressurization of life's changes and challenges. A black diamond may not shine in the same brilliance as a traditional diamond, but it doesn't have to be shiny to know its inherent worth, value, beauty, and divinity.

This is my journey of Surrender, Trust, and Faith in myself, my soul, my wild Divine Feminine, and opening my heart to the essence of God and Spirit alive and awake in all of life. This is my journey Home.

About Paulina Smith

Paulina Smith, known as the Therapeutic Priestess, is a compassionate soul guide and community weaver bridging between psychology and spirituality. With more than ten years of clinical experience as a psychotherapist and four years as a priestess of the divine feminine arts, Paulina is dedicated to raising human consciousness through heart and soul alignment utilizing integrative psychological frameworks, energy work, and ancient modern esoteric teachings.

After surviving childhood cancer at four years old, experiencing the death of loved ones, and healing through betrayals, addictions, shame, guilt, and traumas, Paulina's enthusiasm for life continues to emerge as her north star and compass to keep her heart open through the many facets of life. Following the birth of her two spirited children, she was awakened to her Divine Feminine soul essence. She began her spiritual journey of undoing, being, and becoming her most soul-embodied and expressed Self. The path of motherhood has challenged every aspect of her being and ignited her path of healing to free herself and her children from generational traumas and societal conditionings. The symbolism in her chapter on motherhood teaches her to embrace the depths of love in the simplest of moments shared with her children.

As the founder and steward of The Rose Wolf spiritual and wellness services, Paulina guides women and mothers through the precipice of change that transpires in life transformations, spiritual awakenings, psychedelic preparation and integration, fertility, pregnancy, and motherhood journeys. Paulina has the gift of attunement as a conscious concierge to meet her beloved clients where they are currently in their healing process and support their expansion of self-love, self-confidence, and passion for their lives as they navigate the natural cycles of life, death, and rebirth.

Paulina's life is a testament to her unique approach and refusal to conform to societal expectations. Breaking free from the conditioned constraints of what life "should" look like, she and her husband, two spirited children, and fur babies embarked on a journey to the Big Island of Hawaii. Their mission: to rewild their human by reconnecting with nature and conscious living. This bold step is a reflection of Paulina's commitment to living a life that is true to her values and beliefs.

Passionate and optimistic, she inspires others to embrace the ceremony of their life. Her soul mission is: "Build It, and They Will Come."

Connect   with   Paulina   at   Website: www.therosewolf.com   or   Instagram: @i_am_paulina_smith

Less than 5% Chance

By Sonja Martinovic

"I feel stuck sharing my story," I said on the phone to my niece, Lidija. She said in her badass and oh-so-loving energy, "Sonja, why don't you go to the cemetery?" A feeling of shock and truth entered my body. I knew I didn't have a good answer for her; I hadn't been to the grave in almost a decade. When the truth hits you, you know.

A big silence dropped on my side. She started laughing and said, "What's up, sis? Why did your voice turn into a whisper all of a sudden, ha?" She knows me like no other, so I made a joke, too. I said, "But it's raining hard," and "But I have so much work to do." We both laughed at my attempt to make lame excuses and knew it would be best for me to go.

I cleared my schedule for the day and headed over to my neighbor to have coffee and borrow her umbrella. While the coffee was pouring out of the machine, I talked to her about how I decided to go to the cemetery and how I felt stuck in my chair. Finally, I stood up and looked out her window; it was pouring out of the sky.

I sprinted to my car, but there was no time to open the umbrella. I jumped in and looked outside the car window. The heaviness of the rain and the increasing tension in my body seemed like an energetic match and felt like a sign from above. It was time to go. Before I turned the key, my brother dropped into my consciousness. I was bickering with him the night before, and I was not entirely in the right, so I called him to apologize with a bit of a chip on my shoulder, but instead, I said, "What are you doing?" He responded, "I have some appointments later this afternoon." What are you doing today?" he asked.

At that moment, all the tension inside exploded into tears. I said, "I am going to the grave in Amsterdam," He said, "Who's grave? Luka's?" I said, "Yes, will you come with me?" It was as if he was waiting for me to finally speak those words. "Absolutely," he said. A heavy weight fell from my chest into my feet. I felt a big relief.

Fifteen years ago, I was pacing in the hospital's waiting room. Praying over and over again, take me, please take me instead; my heart was pounding through my whole body; I was having a panic attack. It was my turn; the doctor hooked me up on the ultrasound and spoke those unimaginable words. I am so sorry; his heart is not beating. The once flickering light of hope, love, and wholeness on the ultrasound screen was now a black hole, and something in me died at that moment, too. I thought I would never feel whole again. My life was in pieces, so the story of polarity unraveled.

I turned my head to the side because I couldn't take the pain to look at who I lost. My first son, the crown on our Love and marriage. Gone, the light, the hope, against all odds, miracle baby almost full term. In this same hospital room, they told us you have less than a 5% chance of ever having kids together.

After traveling to Belgium for years, driving six hours for ten-minute checkups, and carefully curating the nursery, I had to give birth to death.

Some family members said, don't look at the baby; it will traumatize you.

But since I was still alive for some reason, I knew I had the strength, and no one could influence me otherwise. Of course, I would look at him; he was my son, and nobody could talk me out of it. His little hands were in front of his eyes like he didn't want to see this world. I was scared of the intense pain of that moment, and then a Big Wave of Love came over me. I had never felt this level of intensity and polarity in life.

I had never felt more alive.

We are unaware of our future experiences. I did not know I would be blessed with two of the kindest, beautiful, smart, and life-loving kids, with a less than 5% chance. Again, Miracles.

Reminiscing on these memories while driving through the neighborhood I grew up in brought a deep nostalgia, and time seemed to go slower, like a frame-by-frame movie.

When I saw my brother, I felt a sigh of relief because, this time, I didn't have to be strong. I felt it was okay to be seen in my purity of emotion and safety, which, so far, had been very rare in my lifetime. We drove through a crowded Amsterdam with a lot of bicycles on the road, which did not allow us to move forward quickly.

My niece—let's just call her my sister because that's how I have experienced her all my life—said, "Oh, and Soki, buy flowers." There was a tiny flower shop I knew was there. However, I guess the flower shop was closed because of the heavy rainfall. We drove to the garden center, and I felt a little bit of panic in the waiting room while looking for flowers.

After some time, my eyes caught a purple plant. I felt so drawn to it; the irony is that purple is my least favorite color. I mean, things might change, but you haven't caught me in purple yet. I felt so strongly about this plant, so I decided to buy it.

When we arrived at the graveyard, it seemed like an endless search for Luka's grave. Luka, my baby boy, loved to kick my tummy during the World Champions League of football almost 16 years ago.

I cleaned the grave, lit the candle, and placed my purple plant upon the grave. Tears and old stacked and suppressed emotions surfaced while my brother soothed me. After it all settled in, my eyes caught something; call it a manifestation sign. Hundreds of tiny little purple flowers were around his grave; I told my brother, "Andre, can " you believe it? It's only around his grave." We stood there, nailed to the ground and in awe. After I reminisced about our experiences during his passing and our past experiences of that time, As I walked through some of the children's graves, some of them touched me to the core.

I saw what I had achieved and how I felt now in a moment, but it also took me 15 years to reflect on how I felt then and my response to the situation.

I did what I knew best at the time. I worked harder, achieved more, got promotions, and got all the certificates I could get. I worked myself up from senior sales to management positions. I took on any learning opportunities I could grab and got certified as a lean Six Sigma project manager, a coach, and a trainer of the sales academy, all of which would play a role later on when I got fired.

In the years after, I worked for some great international businesses, led excellent key account managers, traveled every six weeks, and had the most amazing connections and luxury stays. I also learned so much about myself.

I also learned about corporate high-management politics and how to deal with them, even with some narcissists in top management positions. A pattern of abuse that I had allowed in my life so many times. Why did I agree with suffering, and how many times did I have to learn the same lesson over and over again?

With all the reminiscing on my experiences and emotions, I arrived home. Meanwhile, my 10-year-old daughter had been on a field trip to Amsterdam that day with my neighbor, who let all the children pick a present and a little plant.

Maja, my daughter, unaware that I had been to the grave said, "Look, Mom, I chose this plant. It has the seeds of the plant 'vergeet me nietjes,' translated as 'forget me not.' I googled it, and to my shock, it was the little purple flowers around my son's grave. My brother and I were flabbergasted. This now felt like a divine message and an orchestration at a higher level.

If I looked at it, this was so familiar. I always manifested; nothing was ever a coincidence.

My mother's sudden passing wasn't a coincidence; my business wasn't a coincidence.

Winning a scholarship to an event in 2019 in the United States wasn't a coincidence. Me, someone who had never won anything, now had won a scholarship to the United States, and this lady manifested a first-class ticket, too.

But there was no first-class experience comparable to what I experienced next. Standing in this big arena, with 13,000 people connected, healing, and working on my nervous system, and then it happened. I had an energy coming over me. A Knowing. I would be sharing my voice in helping other people share their voices, too, and stepping into their power of belief in themselves.

I arrived home, full of power and on cloud 9. That didn't last long; soon, I was back in my everyday environment, surrounded by people in different realities to the one I had just experienced in that Arena. It slapped me out of my vibe. Still, I kept my routines to keep my energy in the consciousness of Knowing, even if my whole environment did not support that.

After six weeks of meditation, one moment five years ago shifted my whole view of the world and the core of my consciousness to one of grace and ultimate fulfillment.

This could never be described in words. I didn't even know what gratitude meant until then. Compassion, oneness, and something that is beyond a courageous feeling. The absence of fear, the full presence and embodiment of Love for self. The greatness. How can I even experience this as a human? That was the big question, but I was too present to be stuck in my mind for even a second.

I will never find the words to describe that feeling and what happened after. The next day, I ran into the book *Think and Grow Rich*, and I had read it multiple times, but since that moment, anything I've read isn't simply coincidence; it's guided by Infinite intelligence, up to the point I couldn't handle the inspirations, guidance, and ideas anymore. I was not ready. A big journey of healing took part of my life. Even starting my beautiful business felt like an infinitely guided thing to do. There is so much beauty in the polarity if you surrender to Life.

When we look back on every big adversity, there is a seed of equivalent magic. Understanding is always in the rearview mirror.

My business was no coincidence. Next to my high-performance coaching business, I also launched a podcast, unlocking your success and fulfillment. All of it was guided and made no marketing sense, specifically the name The Vault. The Vault represents that we have the Greatness and all we desire inside; we just need the right combination at the right time. The energy of knowing it would be successful trumped every possible strategy. We launched right in the top 5% of most popular podcasts worldwide; at this moment of writing the Chapter, it is in the top 1.5% worldwide. I know this is only the beginning of something Greater.

Fulfilling your purpose is not easy, and I believe nothing happens without a reason. I had many storms to weather, but these experiences shook me to the core. It also allowed me to unleash trapped emotions and deeply understand who I am and what limitations I took from other people and my environment.

Now, I am the creator of my life, expressing my voice and fulfilling my purpose of helping other people follow their calling because then we can have a beautiful ripple effect on the quality of people's lives.

I realized that success and fulfillment are personal; there is a way, technique, structure, practice, and success energy available authentically for everyone, but it all starts in the true acceptance and love for oneself, the faith it is available for you and knowing that once you obtain and learn to embody the different energies, IS part of your success and fulfillment.

It can not help but manifest itself abundantly to you and others, creating wholeness.

My story matters. Your story matters. We can create in such a powerful way. Our stories change lives.

About Sonja Martinovic

Sonja Martinovic is a high-performance and leadership coach combining transformational sciences and sustainable business practices to support mission-driven entrepreneurs in operating at their highest level with more ease, alignment, and authenticity.

After her own high-level corporate career plunged her into a rude awakening of success and achievement without fulfillment, she found, through divine synchronicities, a higher level of energy and creation and decided to double down on unlocking and unraveling those secrets. She spent the last five years studying the polarity between successful entrepreneurs with and without fulfillment and found the key is in inner transformation.

Her experience and studies in leadership, team management, business development, and needle movers like emotional intelligence, peak performance, quantum physics, neuroscience, and consciousness led her to discover and develop techniques and frameworks. She specializes in simplifying choices that serve the business and personal growth through the lens of focus, energy, and personal power to support the implementation of a winning strategy. The bottom line is she supports high-level CEOs and entrepreneurs to powerfully grow and expand their businesses and lives to fit their own alignment, values, and energy but specifically into finding the Voice in their calling so that the work done through purpose has a ripple effect in improving the quality of people's lives.

Sonja has an 18-year history in international sales management as a sales trainer for Fortune 500 companies and is a certified coach. She is an executive contributor for Brainz500 magazine and a proud host of the top 1.5% of most popular podcasts worldwide, *"The Vault with Sonja Martinovic."* She helps others Launch and share their Voice through podcasting, too. Her biggest wealth is her daughter Maja and her son Maksim.

Connect with Sonja at Website: www.sonjamartinovic.com or Podcast: The Vault with Sonja Martinovic (Spotify and iTunes)

Embracing Emergence - A Journey of Self-Discovery and Healing

By Tina Marie Knittel

In the vast tapestry of existence, we find ourselves entwined between the delicate threads of emergence and the familiar weight of routine. It's a dance, an intricate choreography of awakening and surrender, each movement a step closer to understanding the essence of our being. For me, this dance of emergence has been a lifelong journey, a pilgrimage of self-discovery and healing that spans decades.

Emergence, to me, is more than just a fleeting moment of insight—it's a profound shift in consciousness, a transformative awakening that reshapes the contours of our reality. It's a whisper from the universe, a gentle nudge urging us to shed the layers of illusion and embrace the truth of who we are.

My journey of emergence began long before I even knew what it was. It started in the quiet corners of my childhood, where I first began to feel the weight of unworthiness pressing down upon me like a heavy cloak. From a tender age, I carried within me a sense of inadequacy, a belief that I was somehow flawed and undeserving of love and acceptance.

The roots of this belief stretched deep into the soil of my family history, entwining themselves with the tangled strands of generational trauma. Divorce was a specter that haunted my family, marking my parents as pioneers in a lineage plagued by fractured relationships. I remember the Christmas gatherings, the bittersweet symphony of joy and longing that filled the air as my sister and I watched our cousins receive gifts from extended family members. In contrast, we received only from our father and grandparents. It was a subtle yet poignant reminder of our perceived unworthiness, a wound that cut deeper with each passing year.

As I grew older, the weight of this belief only grew heavier, casting a shadow over every aspect of my life. It manifested in my relationships, career, and even my relationship with myself. No matter how hard I tried, I couldn't shake the feeling that I was somehow fundamentally flawed, unworthy of love and acceptance.

Yet, amidst the darkness, there were moments of light—glimmers of hope that pierced through the veil of despair and reminded me of the inherent beauty of my being. During these moments of emergence, I caught fleeting glimpses of my true self, free from the constraints of fear and self-doubt. These moments were rare and fleeting, like stars in the night sky, but they left an indelible mark on my soul, igniting a spark of hope that refused to be extinguished.

One such moment occurred during a transformative retreat in March. Nestled amidst the tranquil embrace of nature, I found myself among kindred spirits, gathered together in pursuit of wisdom and enlightenment. As the designated healer for the group, I embarked on this journey with an open heart and a willingness to serve.

The days unfolded like pages in a sacred manuscript, each one revealing new insights and revelations. As I communed with the natural world in the quiet spaces between sessions, I felt a profound sense of connection—a reminder that we are all part of something greater than ourselves. During one of these moments of communion, the realization dawned upon me like the first light of dawn—I had been rejecting rejection.

The words echoed in the chambers of my mind, resonating with a truth that had long been buried beneath layers of doubt and uncertainty. I had spent so much of my life running from rejection, avoiding it at all costs, that I had failed to see the more profound truth hidden within its embrace.

I realized rejection was not a condemnation of my worthiness or a reflection of my value as a person. It was simply a part of life, a natural byproduct of being human. And in my efforts to avoid it, I had been denying myself the opportunity for growth and self-discovery.

As I delved deeper into the labyrinth of my own psyche, I began to uncover the source of my self-doubt. It lay in the tangled web of my family history, in the legacy of pain and trauma that had been passed down through generations. Divorce was just one piece of the puzzle, a symptom of deeper wounds that had never been fully healed.

However, as the years passed and I embarked on my own journey of self-discovery, I began to see the patterns that had shaped my life. Through courses, certifications, and countless hours of introspection, I started to unravel the tangled threads of my past, slowly piecing together the fragments of my identity.

Yet, despite my growing understanding of myself and my place in the world, there remained a stubborn resistance—a refusal to fully embrace myself, flaws and all. It was a rejection born of fear, a fear of not being enough, of not measuring up to some arbitrary standard of perfection.

As I journeyed through life, navigating the complexities of adulthood and parenthood, I found solace in the pursuit of knowledge and growth. I threw myself into my work, pouring my heart and soul into every endeavor, yet always keeping my achievements close to my chest, afraid to let others see the depth of my ambition and passion.

I was forced to confront my resistance head-on during that fateful retreat in March. Surrounded by a community of kindred spirits, I was held in a space of unconditional love and acceptance, where my fears and insecurities were met with compassion and understanding.

As we shared our stories and struggles in the warm glow of the firelight, I felt a shift within myself—a loosening of the tight grip that fear had held on my heart for so long. In that moment of surrender, I could finally see myself for who I truly was a being of infinite worth and potential, deserving of love and acceptance just as I am.

In embracing my emergence, I embraced myself fully, with all my flaws and imperfections. I let go of the need for external validation, knowing that my worthiness came from within. As I stepped boldly into the next chapter of my journey, I did so with a newfound sense of purpose and confidence, knowing that whatever challenges lie ahead, I am more than capable of overcoming them.

As I pen these words, I do so with a sense of gratitude for the journey that has brought me to this moment. Each twist and turn, triumph and setback, has shaped me into the person I am today—a person unafraid to embrace her own emergence and step boldly into the light of her own truth.

With Divine Love, Tina Marie

About Tina Marie Knittel

Tina Marie serves as a Midwife for Love. With expansive training in diverse spiritual and holistic practices, Tina Marie weaves together a tapestry of wisdom to guide individuals toward transformation and enlightenment.

With her extensive knowledge and experience, Tina Marie is a versatile guide, tailoring programs to help clients tap into a realm of existence they may not yet comprehend. Her diverse background in Neuro-Linguistic Programming, Reiki healing, and spiritual and life coaching equips her to support each individual on their unique path of self-discovery and healing.

As a miracle-minded intuitive, Tina Marie empowers her clients to trust in divine timing and embrace the present moment fully. She has an innate ability to identify when her clients are stuck in an ego-minded state and gently guides them toward a more loving and authentic perspective.

Tina Marie's remarkable talent lies in her ability to recognize when clients are trapped in cycles that do not reflect their true selves. With her guidance, she helps them break free from these patterns, rediscover their authentic selves, and open up a world of new possibilities they never knew existed.

Tina Marie is a beacon of light in the realm of personal growth and spiritual awakening, beckoning those ready to step into their true potential. She is not just prepared; she is a guiding force, offering a profound opportunity for individuals to embrace love, healing, and self-discovery.

Find   and   connect   with   Tina   at Website: www.loveguidesme.com   or Facebook: @TinaMarieLoveGuidesMe   or   Instagram: @tinamarie.loveguidesme or TikTok: @loveguidesme

The Secret About Dying

By Tori Packer

The hot water cascaded down my back as I lay on the shower floor in the fetal position. I desperately wanted the epidural to alleviate some of the pain, but with each examination, the midwife told me my cervix was not dilated enough. "How?" I thought. "How can this only be the beginning?"

As I lay in the hospital bed, I found myself vomiting from pain and fainting back into the pillow, allowing it to catch me between each contraction, while my tears rolled down my cheeks with anticipation for what was coming again in the next 6-8 minutes.

I was induced at 9 am the day before.

It was now 4 am the following morning.

I was physically and mentally defeated and exhausted. My baby was stuck. My cervix was barely opening. And my body collapsed into a pile of tears. I cried heavy tears. And I begged for relief. I didn't feel empowered or primal at all. I felt like my body had failed me.

Time passed, and the anaesthetist arrived, administering an epidural so I could rest.

Finally, with a long, exhausted exhale, I could. However, the intervention slowed my labor to a standstill, and my cervix stopped dilating at all. At this point, I didn't care. I had disconnected from what was happening, and all I wanted was relief. My body seemed to physically give up.

Oxytocin (a synthetic hormone that stimulates contractions,) an episiotomy, a 3rd-degree tear, a vacuum cup to assist in the birth, 24 hrs, and a team of doctors and nurses helping me, my baby was finally earth side.

I cried.

Not because I was overwhelmed with a sense of euphoria like society promised me (that came later). I cried because I was relieved it was over. I cried because I didn't have to push anymore. I cried as I felt a wave of anxiety envelop me, feeling the immense responsibility of being a mother. My inner dialogue spiraled: "How can I be a mother if I can't even give birth." The doctors in the room wouldn't have noticed. I smiled like I knew I was meant to and passed the tears off as happy tears.

Then, I lay there. Three long hours passed while my physical trauma was stitched back up, literally from the inside out. I joke that it was like CSI-*Vagina*—the beat of the theme song cycling in my mind. Sometimes, humor helps me. But it would take a lot longer to stitch up what had happened to me mentally.

I began my journey into motherhood with the nurses checking on me around the clock. Little did we know, my physical trauma was far from over.

"We need to take her to ICU," I overheard the specialist say to my mum and husband. This was the moment my world would change forever, though I didn't know it then. An aggressive infection was engulfing my entire body. My stitches were breaking down, and I was in septic shock. I would learn later that Sepsis is the body's extreme response to an infection and is a life-threatening medical emergency.

I had failed at doing the one thing I had always believed was a feminine truth: giving birth to life. Looking back, it's poetic to realize that my body gave birth to not only my beautiful baby boy but also me. But it would be years before I understood this wholly.

I was on a cocktail of antibiotics intravenously. But I wasn't responding to any of them. My body didn't do anything I had read about on blogs, watched on social media, or learned about in my perinatal classes. And for a long time, it haunted me that I was robbed of the beautiful right of passage I expected as a new mother.

The doctors all had their poker face on. Later, I learned that even my mum, who had been a GP for over 40 years and trained in obstetrics, was sick with worry. Things weren't looking good. And if it weren't for Western medicine, I most certainly would have died.

Another 24 hours would pass in the ICU before I began to respond somewhat to the antibiotics. And I would spend the next week in the hospital as I started my baptism of fire into motherhood.

My body had been in shock for so long that I had lost any milk that had come in. My breastfeeding journey was now shielded in a dark cloud of hopelessness. I tried to get my milk back. I followed exactly what I was told to do. I pumped. I fed. I massaged my boobs like a cow. I ate the cookies. I drank the tea. All while my baby screamed.

I couldn't sit properly because of the wound and the stitches. I had to bathe every time I went to the toilet to keep the area clean. I couldn't breastfeed because I had lost my milk. I sunk into a deep state of fight or flight.

Most people hate hospitals, but I felt safe there. I didn't trust my own body. I didn't trust myself. I was scared to go home.

As I lay there on the rubber mattress of the hospital bed, heavy tears rolled down my face as I tried to feed through the pain of cracked and bleeding nipples. For the first time in my 32 years, I heard a whisper,

"You are so much more than your physical body.

Your body is simply a vessel. You are a soul. You are infinite love."

For the past 32 years, I have very much been living in the human realm—the 3D. And just momentarily, I peered through a window into the reality that was waiting for me. But I wouldn't recognize it until years later.

My baby had Gastroesophageal Reflux. He would scream from hunger. But would also scream from being fed. His stomach acid was burning away at his esophagus.

The one blessing from being in the hospital for so long was the nurses recognized this was not normal. He couldn't be put down on his back. Ever. Not to change a nappy. Not to have a bath. And definitely not to sleep. I can still hear the blood-curdling screams ringing in my ears eight years later.

So, despite the glimpse of the spiritual awakening waiting for me, I was deep in survival mode. I shut down any communication with my intuition and simply fought to get through each day.

Eighteen months later, my second baby was born. And, as messages often come in patterns, this experience was also shrouded in illness and weeks in hospital.

"There is more than the human body." I heard again.

I recognized the feeling of a safe, warm hug. And for a brief moment, I anchored into the comfort of knowing that it was all going to be OK. But that's all it was- a fleeting moment. Survival mode kicked back in, and doctors prodded and probed, checking oxygen levels. I would be shocked right back into the reality of what was unfolding before my very eyes.

I now had two babies to care for: a curious 18-month-old and a very sick tiny little baby.

By the time my third baby came along, I was almost unrecognizable. I hadn't slept properly in four years. My husband and I were in a tight financial bind, and my nervous system was so frazzled, so heightened, I could barely make simple decisions.

The beautiful life overflowing with peace, joy, ease, and spaciousness that I had envisioned so clearly for myself and my family was a distant memory.

In a serendipitous moment, as we were sharing our third coffee of the day, a friend mentioned to me a beautiful lady she had recently visited called Margaret. She described her ethereal presence to me, her calming energy, and how much Margaret had helped her.

I translated this in my own brain to " Margaret is a psychic." And for some reason, at this moment, I was utterly mesmerized by my friend's story. I had never been to a psychic. I had never even played with the idea that there was more to life than the 3D world. But here I was, hanging off every word she was saying.

In an instant, in what can only be described as time traveling into a vortex, I was right back in that hospital bed, hearing once more...

"You are so much more than your physical body. Your body is simply a vessel. You are a soul. You are infinite love."

And I knew, without a shadow of a doubt, that I had to visit Margaret.

Two weeks later, a two-hour drive from my hometown, I received a two-hour session from Margaret. 222. Looking back, I'm not surprised in the slightest.

It was not at all like I was expecting. In my vision, I had imagined Margaret wearing a long gold gown, she would place her hands on a crystal ball, and tell me all about my future of winning the lotto, much like the scene with Whoopi Goldbug, Patrick Swayze, and Demi Moore in the film *Ghost*.

But instead, there was no crystal ball. Margaret wore all white, and the room had the most calming, tranquil energy. I anchored into a gentle, peaceful state from the moment I entered her presence. I hadn't felt peace like this in years. I felt like I was home. Home to a deep knowing of myself. Of my truth. Of my purpose.

In hindsight, Margaret was not a psychic at all. She was a healer and a reiki master. And she opened my heart to a whole new world of possibility. Finally, I understood and wholly embodied the message that there was more to living than what our five human senses could show us.

Six months later, my entire world crumbled when my Dad was diagnosed with lung cancer. My beautiful Dad. The rock in our family. Our foundation. Our safety. The one person who we would turn to for anything and would make us feel like it would all be ok. Now, he was not OK.

In one five-minute phone call, my dad broke the news. And in that very moment, the past four and a half years flashed before my eyes and finally made absolute sense. Once more, I was thrust straight back into that vortex in the hospital room, hearing *there was more to life than our physical bodies.*

In an instant, I deeply understood why I had to navigate such a difficult journey into motherhood. It was so I could fully embody the belief that there was more to living than the "living."

I carried my family through confusion and disbelief. Assuring them, and him, that he will absolutely, without a shadow of a doubt, always be with us; that nothing can separate us. And I know deep in my core that my 6th sense was opened for a reason.

"I'll miss you," he said as he clasped my hand and closed his eyes.

"No, you won't," I whispered back.

I knew that at that moment, Dad, a doctor for nearly 50 years with a deeply rooted belief system of science, tangible data, and the 3D world, didn't understand what I meant.

For 62 days straight, I laid an altar next to Dad's bedside and offered fresh fruit and flowers to his spirit guides. I came out of the "spiritual closet" to my family and friends at a time I was already at my utmost vulnerable. I decided to own my truth. Own my technicolor. Own what I knew deep down, in the depths of my soul, to be MY calling.

I was certainly not fearless. We're not meant to be. We are here to experience the whole beautiful spectrum of human emotions. But I leaned in anyway. Because that's the thing about intuition and being radically authentic. It's not always without fear, but it is with absolute faith that there can be no other way.

When you truly step into yourself, your power, your most radically authentic truth, you become magnetic.

Eighteen months passed in what felt like 18 seconds.

And my favorite person in the world, my Dad, left his body.

But I was awakened.

And I knew there was so much more to living than the living.

About Tori Packer

Tori Packer is Australia's leading intuition and manifestation coach. A powerhouse in the manifestation world, she is known for changing the lives of women around the globe by guiding them to fully trust their inner wisdom so that they can manifest a life more magical than their wildest dreams.

Originally a primary school teacher and then a savvy social media coach who built a large following by cutting through the noise and creating a community of women who embraced her authenticity, Tori now uses this platform for her life's soul work.

After the birth of her boys and the baptism of fire into motherhood, Tori's life took a profound turn. She was awakened to the world of intuition, a journey that was further intensified by the passing of her dad, her hero. This life-altering experience thrust her into following her life's true purpose, to help thousands of women live a life in alignment with their soul's purpose and manifest their dream life of fulfillment and abundance.

Tori's life is a beautiful balance of the 'extra' and the simple. She manifests her worldly travels and a life beyond her wildest dreams (with five overseas holidays - three which were all expenses paid - in the last year). Yet, she also cherishes the simple life, like backyard BBQs with her family and friends in her small Australian country town, showing that abundance and fulfillment can coexist with simplicity and joy.

Tori is here to see you elevate every facet of your life. You can follow and connect with her at

Connect with Tori at Instagram: @tori.packer

Seeing the Sacred

By Dr. Tricia Working

Blood was dripping down my arm from a savage sacred tiger's kiss. His paws were poised to kill yet holding me ever so softly, tugging me until I could find myself and my life; he was holding my jagged edges and licking my tears into forever.

I have returned and emerged from the darkness many times. Just this Easter, I was lying in a hospital bed, loving invisible anchors wrapping around me, holding me firmly, grounding me because it was not yet my time; not that I wasn't ready, just caught off guard momentarily; no, it's not time yet.

Before I even think about Easter, I need to go back to the beginning, where everything truly started for me and my soul.

Refuge, the sanctuary in a tiger's paw; I am drawn into this new identity being forged from the scattered ashes of my broken self - first blood drawn - first kiss - my blood on Tear's nose. I didn't feel the bite, only the blood as they breathed life into me - it made me feel as though I was on the edge of my life.

The tigers showed me the truth of my soul without reservation, the sacredness I had never been allowed to see, keep, or be forced to hide. They unleashed it and held the space for me to explore and travel the layers and depths within. They claim me as one of their own, opening a portal, a dimension in time, a way of being that brought me fully into the expansion that I've never known existed within me.

Words to find the experience of the tigers' touch, to be with them, to be as they are, to be with them knowing they could kill me just as easily as they kiss me, to lie beside them knowing there is only a fence between us. Their paws reaching through and beneath to hold my hands, slather my face with harsh kisses, to be in Twilight with the Tigers, to feel the magic of the night, their breath, the sound that emanates from deep within responding with the primality locked in, with moments too sacred to share.

Words feel almost too empty to describe the profound connection between beast and woman, the ancient majesty, eternal life, and the symbolic energy of life. The Tigers' touch brings me to a higher level within. It is at this moment but more than this moment—an eternity of two collapsed into one, defining and revealing the ultimate sense of self, past and future merge. Questions become answers, and questions become knowing, yet I keep them sacred, savored, and treasured. Beyond man, myself, and my raw edges, I am drawn into this new identity. I can only admit to the need to be here with them—experiencing them on a level beyond words—denying description yet deeply known by my heart reunion communion.

What drew me here this time, what brought me to the Tigers, and what did they have to tell me? They bring me peace, my soul Quest. They look at me as if Humanity does not. They see the depth, the hunger, the longing. They make me feel I belong just as I am. Their passion, play, and power show me a dangerous place within, an escape to a former life. I feel I have the soul of animals, especially the big cats. I dream of ancient times when I roamed with them and lived a Kiplingesque life. I was lucky to make friends with a gal associated with an exotic animal sanctuary specializing in tigers and big cats, and I would spend time with them. I would come home at times bruised, a bit bloody from their hugs and kisses, dirty and disheveled but with complete joy and abandon.

Rick, my husband, would always be afraid that I would get eaten by the tigers. I would simply say that that would be my desired way to go. Everything was different when I was with the Tigers. Can you imagine being face to face with them, looking directly into their eyes, feeling their hot breath on your face, with their paws grasping to hold and hug you? They would jump on my back, the Lords of the jungle and their ancient majesty gazing at me with such depth and emotion. Yes, they absolutely would bite and scratch me, and yes, they drew blood. But I truly never felt it, and it was never done to harm me because I was accepted as one of their own.

I could feel in every moment their love and the totality of who they were and what they could reach within me that I did not fully understand was there until I was with them. There were depths within me that were only accessible through the tigers. They brought up what I had been waiting my whole life for. To be felt, understood, and experienced in my wholeness. It took the passion, power, rawness, and ferocity of who they were to show me that same sovereignty lay within me.

I wasn't aware of it; they showed me where, why, and what my jagged edges were and that there was power to that. They showed me the soft, secret, and sacred places hidden beneath all my childhood wounds. Beneath the abuse, the failure of my family to see me, understand, or recognize my essence, and instead tried to force and shape me to be that perfect version, which, of course, I became because that's what you do, especially as a daughter of t he South.

The Tigers gave me back or gave me to myself; they, like my Grandfather, saw me, saw my essence, and accepted me. They were the WayShowers of my soul and helped strengthen and empower me. Let's be very real; if you think about it, how many people in the entire world ever in their lifetime have the opportunity to truly engage in real life 1-on-1 with the truth of the Tiger or any of the magnificent big cats, truly engaged with their hearts and their souls?

I know not many people want to or would take the chance if they had it. It's not everyone's dream, but it expanded me. Each fight, bruise, scratch, and kiss—being wrapped in their arms, having them jump on my back and nuzzle me with their heads, even sleeping beside them through the bars and having their paws cup my hands in theirs—was a life-altering moment. All of these experiences changed me forever.

So, as I said, big cats captured my soul, but the little cats captured my heart. While I grew up believing myself to be a dog person because we raised, trained, and showed dogs all my life, I realized when I got my first cat at age 25 that I was actually a cat person. The truth is that the real lessons of life I didn't learn from people; I learned them from the Animal Kingdom. The gifts, insights, and much of my spirituality came through my work with the animals. I have been blessed over the years with the animals who have come to me personally - so many of them have been highly evolved beings. Throughout my life, they have reincarnated back to me over and over again to continue the spiritual work with me and to take me deeper into understanding aspects of consciousness and spirituality, especially the work that I do with the transition of life and grief. They have been the greatest teachers.

One of the most sacred experiences I've ever been gifted was during the transition of one of my most precious animals, my Treasure Map. During the moments that his soul was finally leaving his body as he was in my arms, I was able to see his soul rise from his body and make its way up to Heaven. This beautiful, iridescent outline of his body was wafting softly, slowly to the top of the ceiling, through it, and into the heavens. It was both transformative and transcendent. My heart could barely breathe or beat; it felt like I had been given that gift because my entire relationship with Treasure Map was wrapped in love. Sometimes, however, there are mixed and missed signals in my relationships with the animals.

We make agreements about how much we can love each animal that comes to us. At times, I have made judgments against myself because some of my pets love me so completely, and I could not love them back at the same level. I met judgments about loving one animal more than another. I always felt an ache in my spirit for my perceived lack through the lessons my animals afforded me. Yet, I came to understand that it is not about judging the animals or myself but about honoring the truth of my relationship with them. Spirit is now asking us to move into a new level of consciousness and awareness regarding animals. Each animal that comes into our lives or crosses our path has done so for a specific reason, and it is our job in our spiritual search to seek out the lessons.

One of the more difficult lessons is to understand that we carry within us the capacity to love in many layers and degrees - we do so with each other, but even more so with the animals. I have found that much of our love is unconscious, and we're now being asked to wake up. I have learned big lessons in this regard because I just couldn't get it into my consciousness the first time around. That is, through all the pain and the power of Spirit, you get opportunities to continue learning until you get it. My first lesson came with Minuet, half-sister to my Shi Tzu Cayce. She came as a temporary favor for a friend and ended up permanent. She was a beautiful girl, just the opposite of Cayce in temperament. She loved everyone, and all she wanted was to be loved. I always felt guilty about her because I could never give her the depth of love she sought from me. I could see it in her eyes that she knew I had only eyes for Cayce. She and Cayce remembered and loved each other and played together, and they both developed the same diseases of the heart and cancer later in life. When she was diagnosed, all my guilt returned. She was so true of spirit that she did not chastise me but still begged for my love - I did much soul-searching and faced a terrible truth - I shied away from Min because she reminded me so much of myself, and I had never made peace with my own deep need to be loved. When I faced that, a new depth of Love opened within me for her, and we talked and spent a lot of time together. I found a more freeing kind of love for her, although I still felt guilt over my stronger connection with Casey. Min's last months were more full and loving than all her years before. However, I still could not forgive myself for not being able to love her more or better before then. She never judged me or turned away, but I turned away from myself.

Another powerful lesson in the depth and layers of love came with Karma's illness – I believed had I been more connected, I would have noticed his illness sooner - as Karma went through his illness, he worked with me on learning to listen to him - one of the many lessons he provided me was in working to continue my life while also still journeying with him. I was always aware of the connection with each of my animals, but I had to face the fact that, in some ways, it was still about me, and that had to change; my heart hurt, too, because I know how Karma loved me and while I truly did love him, for me, there was a difference in depth that I didn't know how to reconcile what I knew and felt. Yet, Karma taught me that not only are there degrees of love for each animal, but there are also different agreements of love with each, and there are no losses as we perceive them.

Of course, animals have feelings and emotions, jealousies and tiffs just as we do, but in reality, their souls are more conscious than ours; they truly get it. They come to the Earth and us, knowing what role they will play and what level of love goes with each relationship. Yet, like us, they get into their egos and get emotional at times. Still, they know and accept the love relationship with us - they know that no relationship can be exactly the same and that what is important are the agreements and the lessons that go with the loving - it is our issues and our stuff that make the love we feel for them not enough or wrong or less than whatever we think it should be though, I was able to face my feelings for Minuet, Karma and to see all my cats more clearly.

So ultimately, in the end, what God, Spirit, and the Universe are trying to show us is that the animals are The Messengers, The Unexpected WayShowers on your spiritual journey, and they're here to help you find your path, forge it, focus on it right, recognize it, and heal it. If you allow, the animals will shape you, soothe you, serve you, and source you in sacred ways you never even think to look for because they are as close to the divine as you can get.

I invite you to take another look at that precious pet you've got, and if you don't have a pet, just the next time you see an animal cross your path look a little longer, and a little harder. Take a moment and allow yourself to see the sacred in them, as they are, but mirrors reflecting the sacred in you.

About Dr. Tricia Working

Dr. Tricia Working is a world-renowned animal mystic, healer, author, speaker, and Ordained Minister, facilitating conscious connections with the animal kingdom as a certified spiritual coach and professional counselor. She leads transformative conversations on how animals serve as guardians of consciousness, calling in a higher awareness and commitment not just to animals, but to humanity.

Tricia believes that spiritual growth, mindset, and paradigm shifts can occur through connection to animals; even our household pets are here to provide guidance. She shares how to incorporate these transformative experiences in her groundbreaking book series, *The Fur Agreements*, and her wildly conscious conversations through *The Epiphany Series*.

Southern, Sassy, and a special kind of spiritual, Dr. Tricia is indeed a cat of many magical colors. She is known globally for her unique understanding of the final moments in life and her loving ability to assist pets and their families with ease and grace as they journey through the final goodbye transition process.

She stands by her promise that once you read her book, you will never see animals in the same way. Dr. Tricia is an Atlanta, Georgia native with seven years of experience in shelter management; she founded Paws for Thought Animal Foundation in 1993 and now lives in the Southern United States with her abundance of furry friends.

You can connect with Dr. Tricia at Website: DrTriciaWorking.com. or email drtriciaw@yahoo.com

About the Publisher

Mosaic Media is not your average publisher.

We do books differently; combining intuitive intelligence and the energetics of becoming an author with proven frameworks and soul-led strategy.

We have created a unique book system, specifically for fempreneurs who know you have a powerful message, divine download, signature method or unique framework, along with the CALLING to publish a book, create iconic impact and leave a legacy you are born for. But you also know you want that book to work FOR you, not just sit on a theoretical shelf.

Our method has all the benefits of traditional publishing (and the bestseller tag if you so desire), AND we set your book up as its own automated marketing channel that runs on autopilot to sell copies and bring in dream clients daily.

For the coaches, leaders, online educators, and facilitators who desire an automated dream client-generating system where your book doesn't just sell a few hundred copies and that's it, but rather sells copies and brings in qualified leads daily.

We understand the gravity of having a calling to share your message with the world.

We know you've got a profound mission, big life experiences, and a powerful story to share. You've always had that niggle to publish your own book, but you've no idea where to start. Maybe that's why you've ended up with this book in your hand....

We work with female leaders who desire to share your message, mission and movement on a global scale.

Is that you?

Visit www.mosaic-media.co to find out more.

Thank you so much for reading our book!

We love hearing your thoughts and would really appreciate feedback! If you could leave us a review would be so helpful!

Please take two minutes by going back to your purchase on Amazon and letting us know what you thought of the book:

Thanks so much!

Georgie and the co-authors of Emergence

www.ingramcontent.com/pod-product-compliance
Lightning Source LLC
Chambersburg PA
CBHW072153090426
42740CB00012B/2246